December –
Christmas 1999

To BOB

with love ♡

from your 'little Cherub'

Mary ♡

ZAFTIG

ZAFTIG

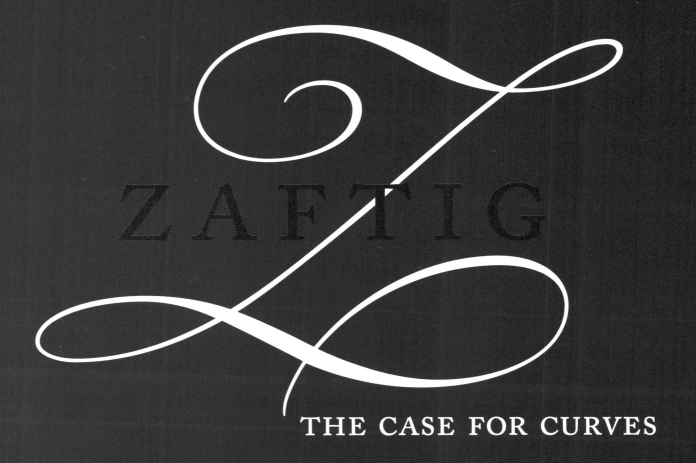

THE CASE FOR CURVES

DARLING & COMPANY 1999

BY EDWARD ST. PAIGE

ISBN 1-883211-16-6

FIRST PRINTING

PRINTED IN SINGAPORE

DARLING &
COMPANY

POST OFFICE BOX 4399
SEATTLE
WASHINGTON 98104

TABLE OF CONTENTS

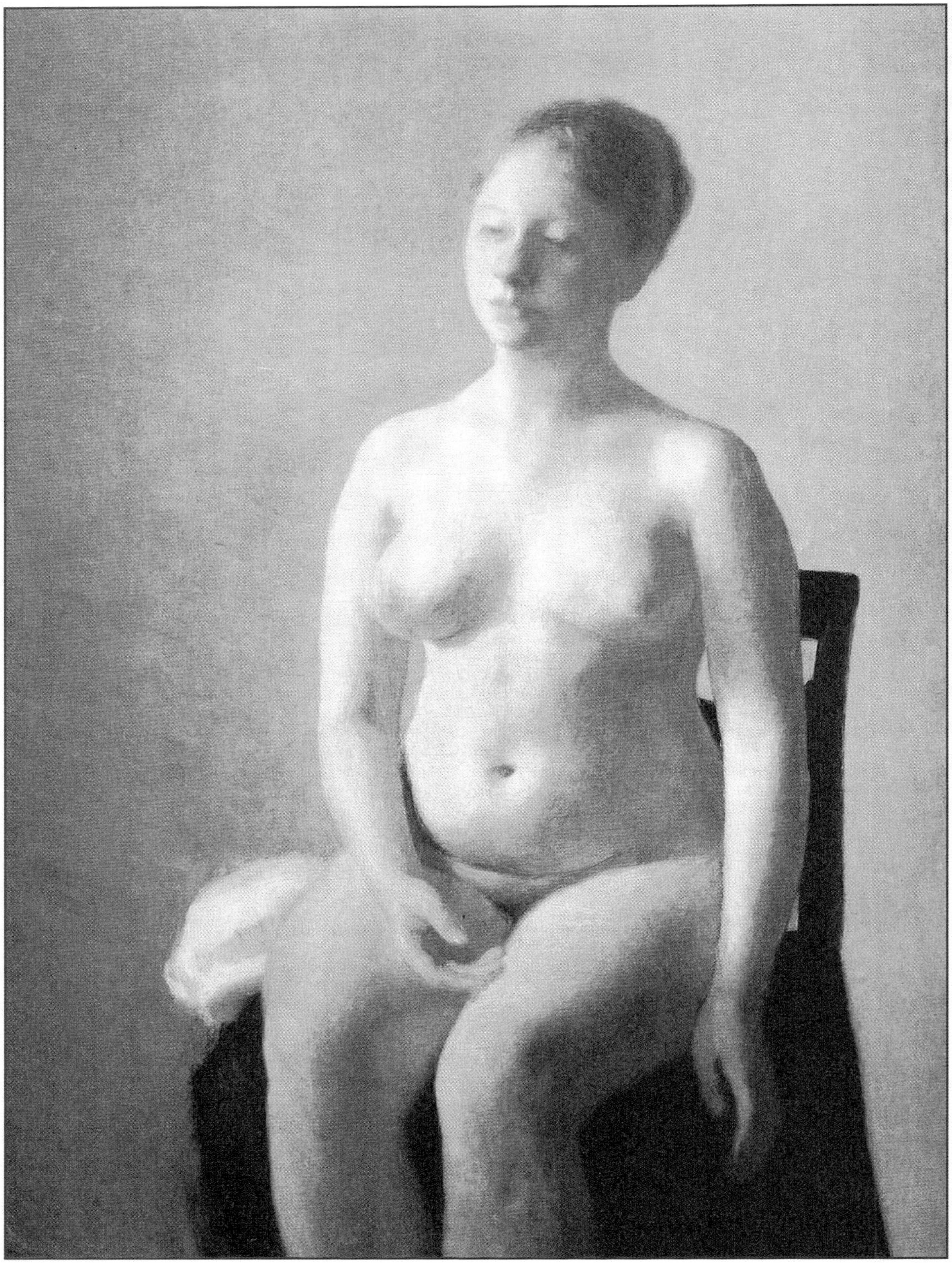

INTRODUCTION

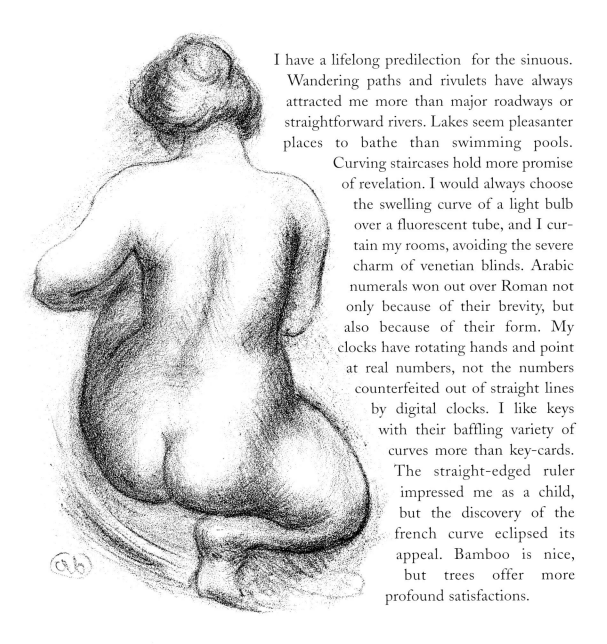

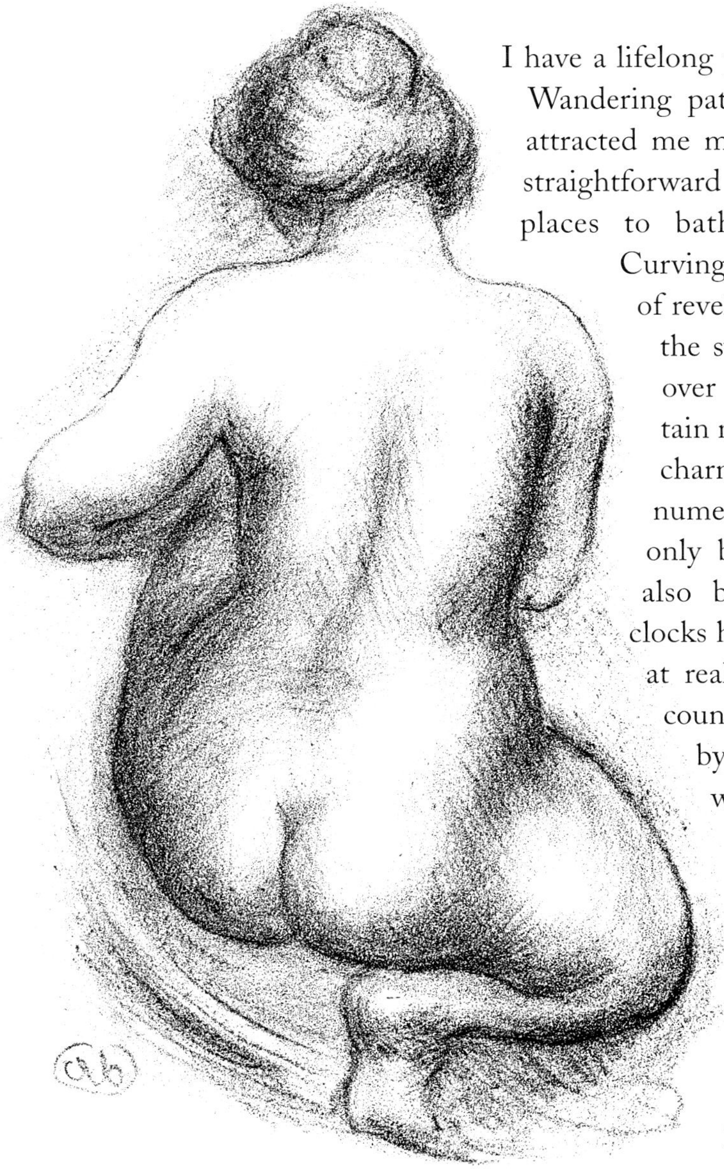

I have a lifelong predilection for the sinuous. Wandering paths and rivulets have always attracted me more than major roadways or straightforward rivers. Lakes seem pleasanter places to bathe than swimming pools. Curving staircases hold more promise of revelation. I would always choose the swelling curve of a light bulb over a fluorescent tube, and I curtain my rooms, avoiding the severe charm of venetian blinds. Arabic numerals won out over Roman not only because of their brevity, but also because of their form. My clocks have rotating hands and point at real numbers, not the numbers counterfeited out of straight lines by digital clocks. I like keys with their baffling variety of curves more than key-cards. The straight-edged ruler impressed me as a child, but the discovery of the french curve eclipsed its appeal. Bamboo is nice, but trees offer more profound satisfactions.

I think this volume will appeal to those with similar enthusiasms.

The tendency of the female body is endomorphism (round and soft), but that has not kept humankind, at various times, from preferring one or another body shape, and using the mysterious force of fashion to promote and reward the prevailing ideal.

As this book will demonstrate, fashion has, in human history, frequently preferred endomorphic women—women with the figure that nature is likely to bestow. There are, however, eras in which other shapes are desired—very narrow shoulders, long necks, tiny ears, huge hips and buttocks, and so on, with almost infinite variety. Dress and costumes are used to create the illusion of conformity, wherever possible. The most tyrannical fashion is thinness, for it cannot be counterfeited, unlike fullness which padding can achieve.

We, at this time, are in a period where a nearly unattainable ideal exists—women are expected to be very thin, and also have a large and protuberant bosom. This combination of contrary traits is very rare; thus most individuals fail to achieve it, with a myriad of unfortunate results.

I dislike this situation and have compiled this volume to counter it, not merely because it is unhealthy, but also because it runs against what clearly is the tendency of the female body. Here we celebrate the beauty of woman in her most natural form.

'Good' and 'better' in respect of beauty are not easy to discern, for it would be quite possible to make two different figures, neither conforming with the other, one stouter, the other thinner, and yet we might scarce be able to judge which of the two excelled in beauty.

Albrecht Dürer from ***Four Books of Human Proportions****, 1528*

The categories of 'fat' and 'thin' are not innate and do not have intrinsic meanings; rather, they are socially constituted, along with definitions of perfection and beauty. Social and cultural representations are central in forming these definitions and in giving meaning to the configurations of the body.

Lynda Nead from ***The Female Nude****, 1992*

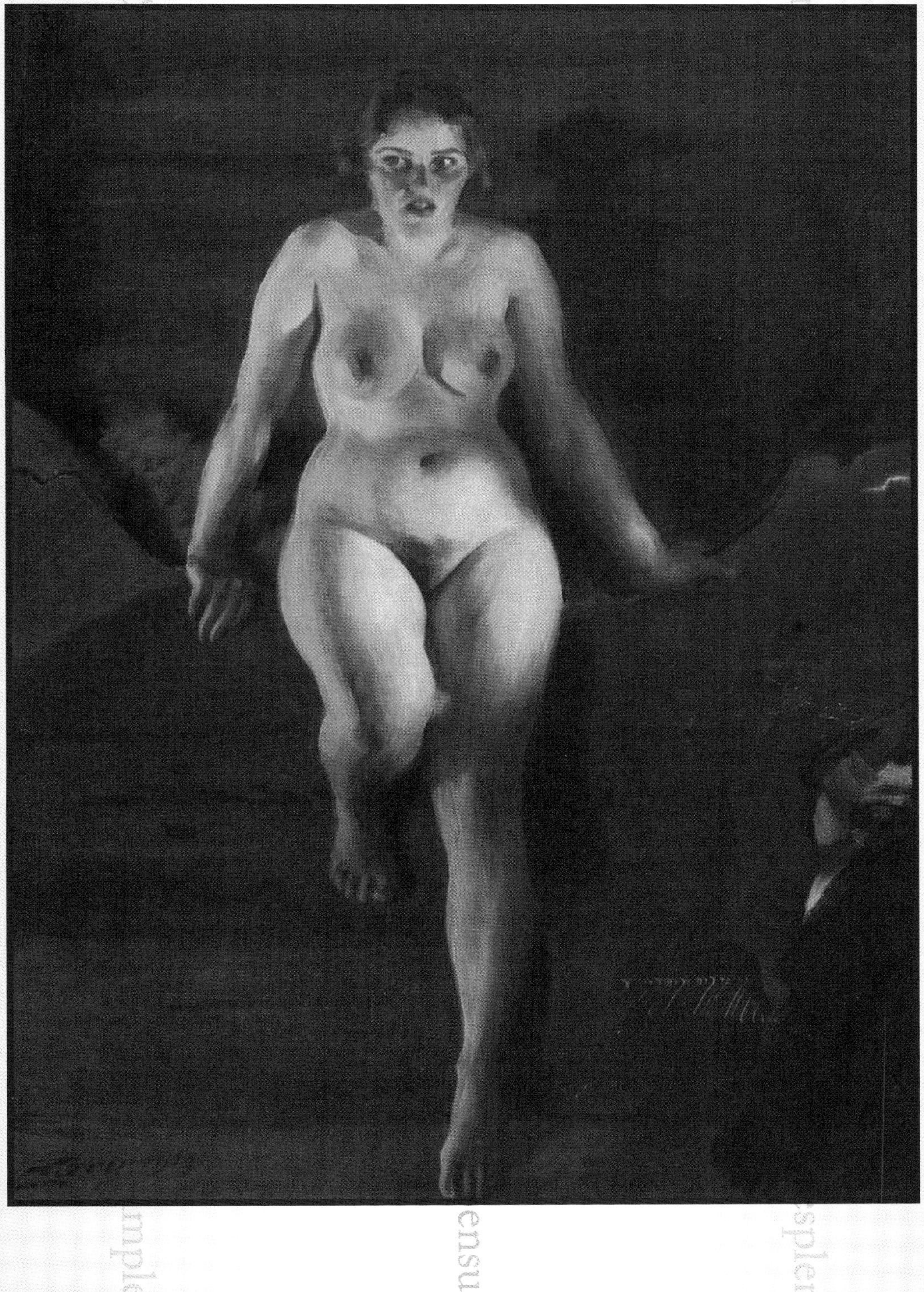

Women can change the cut of their clothes at will, but how can they change the cut of their anatomies? And yet, they have done just this thing. Their shoulders have become narrow and slightly sloping, their throats more slender, their hips smaller and their arms and legs elongated to an extent that suggest that bed, upon which the robber, Procrustes, used to stretch his victims.

Anonymous, 1892

I sent two models on a trip together to do bathing suits. One girl called me and said, "Oh, my God, I wish I was her; she's got such a lean body with perfect muscle tone." And the other one called me up and said, "I was so ashamed of my figure, because she's so womanly."

Monique Pillard

There are fashions in human beauty as there are in clothes and architecture, and the ideal of female fleshiness did not survive the turn of the present century. Of the many changes in public taste and standards that have meanwhile taken place, perhaps none is as thoroughgoing as the change in the publicly canonized version of what constitutes a desirable female body shape.

*Anne Scott Beller from **Fat and Thin**, 1977*

The preference for extreme thinness in women is related to a desire to divorce women from their reproductive role. This tendency is not unique to a modern sensibility, for it has existed in other times (see the Cranach Venus on page 17). For us it began early in our century, reached its apex in the 1920s, and despite a few counterattacks by fullness, it has ruled, almost unchallenged, since then. Kaz Cooke in *Real Gorgeous* suggests several possible motives for the popularity of thinness: a desire for freedom from reproduction; an angry reaction to men's pleasure in flesh; a growing awareness of the health dangers of fatness; retention of the flatness of childhood as a manifestation of a desire not to grow up; a feeling that discipline is a good, which applied to the areas of exercise and diet, leads to slimness; a belief that we have reached a point in civilization where we can, and should, overcome the dictates of nature. Further, she sees several forces acting on women to encourage thinness: the enormous influence of the fashion industry, which through its much disseminated images of impossibly thin models encourages women to resemble the figure which is easiest to dress; and, capitalism, which makes money by encouraging everyone to want what they don't have, and to attempt to become that which they need a lot of help in becoming.

Short, flat, angular and geometric. Feminine dress today follows the lines of a parallelogram, and in 1925 they will certainly not be celebrating the return of the fashion for soft curves with the provocative bust and the luscious haunches…

Colette from ***Vogue*** *magazine, 1925*

In recent years there has been a strong shift towards a mock-juvenile contour, with adult women offering the slim lines of young schoolgirls as a sexual attraction. By omitting the broad child-bearing hips this display suggests athletic fun and sex rather than the heavy responsibility of breeding and the establishment of a family; and by imitating the weaker 'little girl' frame it also signals the subservient immaturity of the juvenile.

Desmond Morris from ***Bodywatching****, 1985*

A sociologist could no doubt give ready answers why embodiments of elegance should take this somewhat ridiculous shape-—feet and hands too fine for honest work, bodies too thin for childbearing, and heads too small to contain a single thought. But elegant proportions may be found in many objects that are exempt from these materialist explanations—in architecture, pottery, or even handwriting. The human body is not the basis of these rhythms, but their victim. Where the sense of chic originates, how it is controlled, by what inner pattern we unfailingly recognize it—all these are questions too large and too subtle for a parenthesis. One thing is certain. Chic is not natural.

Kenneth Clark from ***The Nude****, 1956*

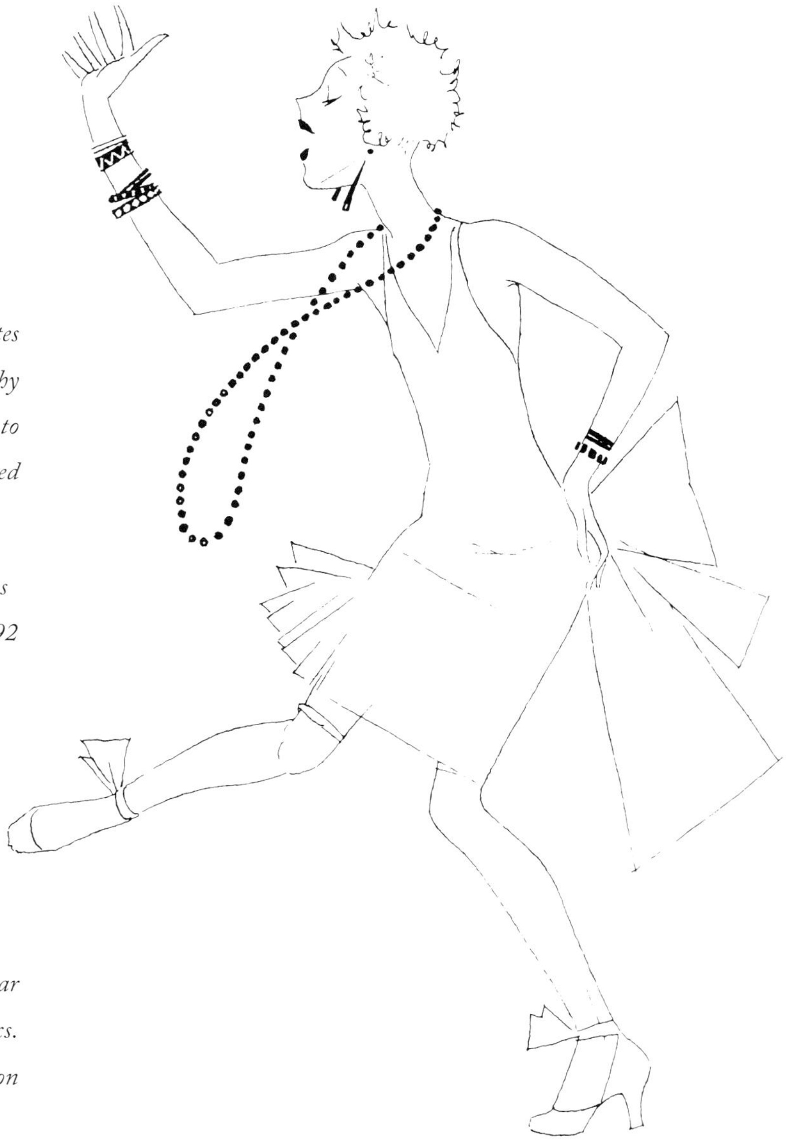

Judging from their work, the designers of fashion-plates are utterly ignorant of anatomy and art. Being so, why should their dictum be heeded upon a subject vital to physical beauty? Like pretensions would be resented from any other craftsmen.

Frances Mary Steele and Elizabeth Steele Adams from ***Beauty of Form and Grace of Vesture****, 1892*

Beauty of the flapper era was notable for the near absence of female secondary sexual characteristics. Women were using rolling machines, iodine, starvation diets, and strenuous exercise to reduce their weight.

April Fallon from ***Body Images****, 1990*

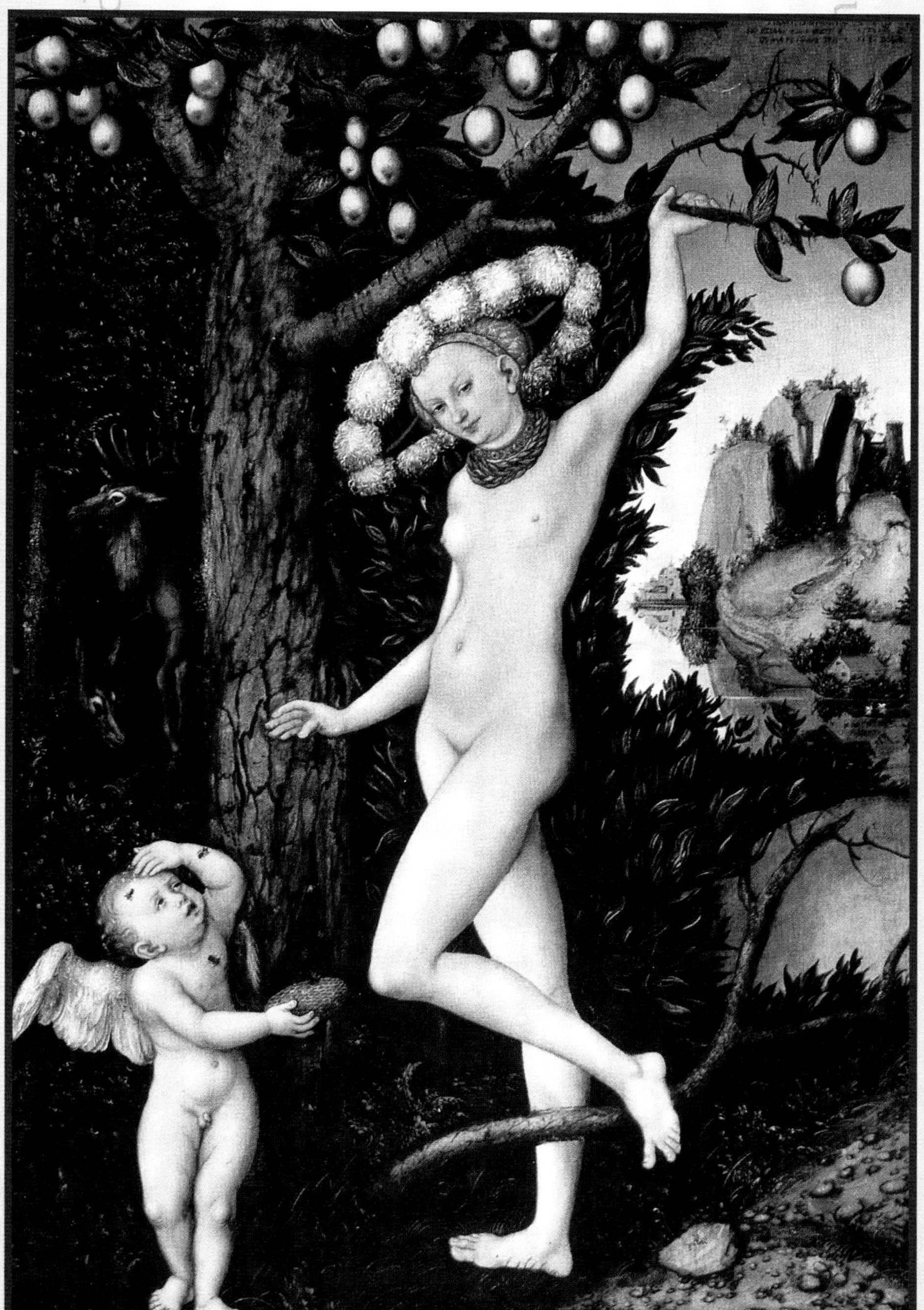

The great clothing fashion designer Paul Poiret, writing in the 1930s, looked back on the change of fashion from the full figured woman to the slim ideal that he helped to create, remembers the earlier time, and regrets the change. "[Raymonde was] as lissome as she was shapely, like they made them at that time....[She] had pretty forms in front and behind (this was still appreciated and in demand at that time). I found in these attractions an infinite charm, and if I had been able to imagine that they were on the point of disappearing, perhaps I would have taken better advantage of them."

Until the 1980s, excess weight was the target of most ads for diet products; today, one is much more likely to find the enemy constructed as bulge, fat, or flab. "Now," a typical ad runs, "get rid of those embarrassing bumps, bulges, large stomach, flabby breasts and buttocks. Feel younger, and help prevent cellulite buildup....Have a nice shape with no tummy." To achieve such results (often envisioned as the absolute eradication of body, as in "no tummy") a violent assault on the enemy is usually required; bulges must be "attacked" and "destroyed," fat "burned," and stomachs (or, more disgustedly, "guts") must be "busted" and "eliminated."

Susan Bordo from ***Unbearable Weight****, 1993*

In 1984...a study conducted by Glamour magazine and analyzed by Susan Wooley and Wayne Wooley revealed that 75 percent of the 33,000 women surveyed considered themselves "too fat," despite the fact that only one-quarter were deemed overweight by standard weight tables, and 30 percent were actually ***underweight.*** *Similar studies followed, some specifically attempting to measure perception of body size, all with the same extraordinary results. A study by Kevin Thompson, for example, found that out of 100 women "free of eating-disorder symptoms" more that 95 percent overestimated their body size—on average one-fourth larger than they really were.*

Susan Bordo from ***Unbearable Weight****, 1993*

There is considerable outrage over the effects of the cult of thinness. Millions of women, confronted by the fashion for thinness, respond with shame, and many torture themselves trying to achieve an ideal beyond their reach.

This work attempts to demonstrate that this cult is not only destructive, but is, additionally, a movement away from the womanly beauty that most women have as their biological heritage. Breasts, stomach, and hips are the visible signs of femininity, and their prominence an important part of attractiveness. The social forces that obscure this simple truth are too complex for full analysis, but many enjoy women with prominent sexual characteristics, and this book is a celebration of them.

Bless your body always. Speak no word of condemnation about it.

Rebecca Beard from ***Everyman's Search***

...these large women inspire no revulsion and feel none for themselves; in these big bodies there is not the slightest trace of self-hatred or shame, suppressed rage or hostility, nothing the least bit pathological, neither hatred for the mother nor extreme antagonism for the self; there is no evidence of emotional distress which drives the woman to eat more than she desires for her pleasure; there is no alienation from the flesh, so that it appears grotesque, either to the beholder, or to the woman-spirit it carries, which is here sensitive and intelligent, masterful, and proud.

Kim Chernin from **The Obsession**, *1981*

It is undeniable that, in drawing and painting, the female body is much more frequently dealt with than the male. This is not only to be explained by the obvious fact that the unclothed woman is usually far more attractive to the artist...It is also true that the female body offers a greater variety of forms and contours to draw, and light and shadow have more differentiated forms and surfaces to define.

George Eisler from **From Naked to Nude**, *1977*

Her [Marilyn Monroe] stomach, untrammeled by girdles or sheaths, popped forward in a full woman's belly, inelegant as hell, an avowal of a womb fairly salivating in seed—that belly which was never to have a child— and her breasts popped buds and burgeons of flesh over many a questing sweating moviegoer's face. She was a cornucopia. She excited dreams of honey for the horn.

Norman Mailer

The curve is more powerful than the sword.

Mae West

The most literal symbolic form of maternal femininity is represented by the nineteenth-century hourglass figure, emphasizing breasts and hips—the markers of reproductive femaleness—against a fragile wasp waist. It is not until the post-World War II period, with its relocation of middle-class women from factory to home and its coercive bourgeois dualism of the happy homemaker-mother and the responsible, provider-father, that such clear bodily demarcation of "male" and "female" spheres surfaces again. The era of the cinch belt, the pushup bra, and Marilyn Monroe could be viewed, for the body, as an era of "resurgent Victorianism." It was also the last coercively normalizing body-ideal to reign before boyish slenderness began its ascendancy in the mid-1960s.

Susan Bordo from ***Unbearable Weight****, 1993*

Marilyn Monroe
and "Niagara"
a raging
torrent of
emotion
that even
nature can't
control!
20th CENTURY-FOX presents
Niagara
TECHNICOLOR
STARRING
MARILYN MONROE · JOSEPH COTTEN · JEAN PETERS
CHARLES BRACKETT · HENRY HATHAWAY · CHARLES BRACKETT, WALTER REISCH RICHARD BREEN

If you have been made on a generous plan, you have qualities that littleness can never possess. Who with any authority has said that slender persons are of the best type? Only carry yourself well, be reposeful and stately, with a brain that sits supremely on the throne of your being, and you may come into your kingdom of power and love.

Frances Mary Steele and Elizabeth Livingston Steele Adams from **Beauty of Form and Grace of Vesture**, *1892*

When University of Texas psychologist Devendra Singh, Ph.D., showed pictures of 12 female shapes to some 700 men from industrialized as well as relatively undeveloped countries, they uniformly rated very thin figures (the kind many women believe they should be struggling to achieve) less attractive than normal, slightly heavier shapes. The men's standard for bodily beauty was based on a low waist-to-hip ratio rather than overall weight. A "normal" size woman whose waist was 70 percent of her hip size (i.e. a 30-inch waist and 43-inch hips) was the universal beauty ideal. This preference, Singh speculates, represents a kind of genetic programming from the distant past, with female curves signaling fertility and health.

Glamour *magazine, 1998*

Thin women seem tense with the effort of resisting their animal nature, of trying to turn themselves into works of art, of struggling against the will of nature.

Heavier women have accepted their residence in a body shaped by the scheme of creation rather than one fashioned by their own wills. Their acceptance of the gift of flesh promises fleshly joys.

When I was young my family, in the course of my father's naval career, frequently made drives across the US, from coast to coast.

The many days of driving through Iowa and Kansas grew wearisome. The sameness, the flatness, staled quickly. But when we approached the Rocky Mountains we all awakened. The hills and mountains offered variety and surprises, and we delighted in the adventure of discovery.

I find no sweeter fat than sticks to my own bones.

Walt Whitman from ***Leaves of Grass****, 1855*

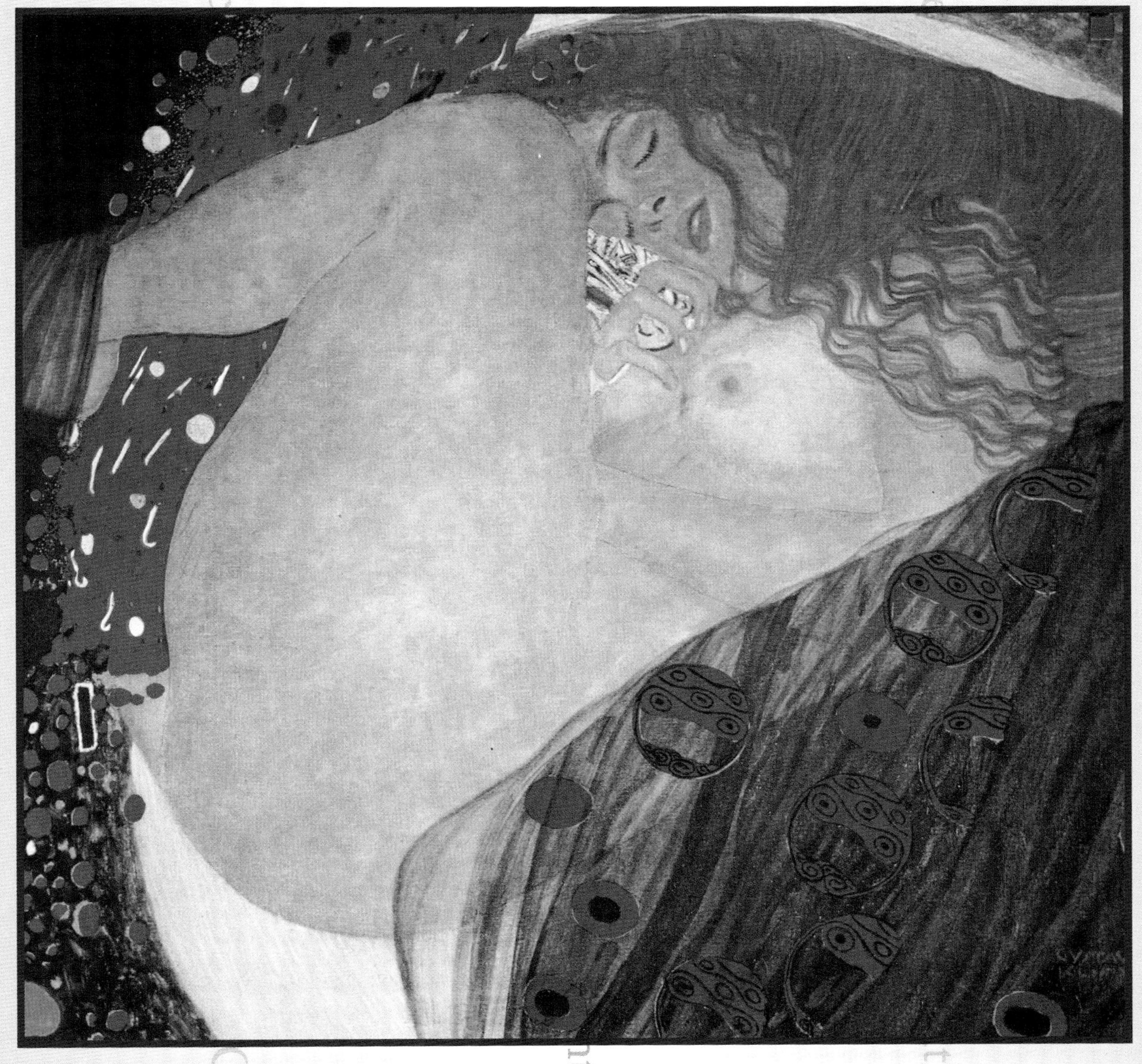

The portrayal of Eve as the first woman, the mother of the human race, is obviously more resonant with meaning than the portrayal of any of her billions of daughters. The artist asks, "What was she like, this prototype of womankind?" In most cases the answer is a full figured woman.

When it comes to women and bodies, God probably said: let there be flesh.

Demetria Martinez,

***National Catholic Reporter**, 1995*

EVE

In *Imaging American Women,* Martha Banta refers to a turn-of-the-century scientist who tried to prove that Eve was 200 feet tall, believing that the original woman needed to be immense.

EVE

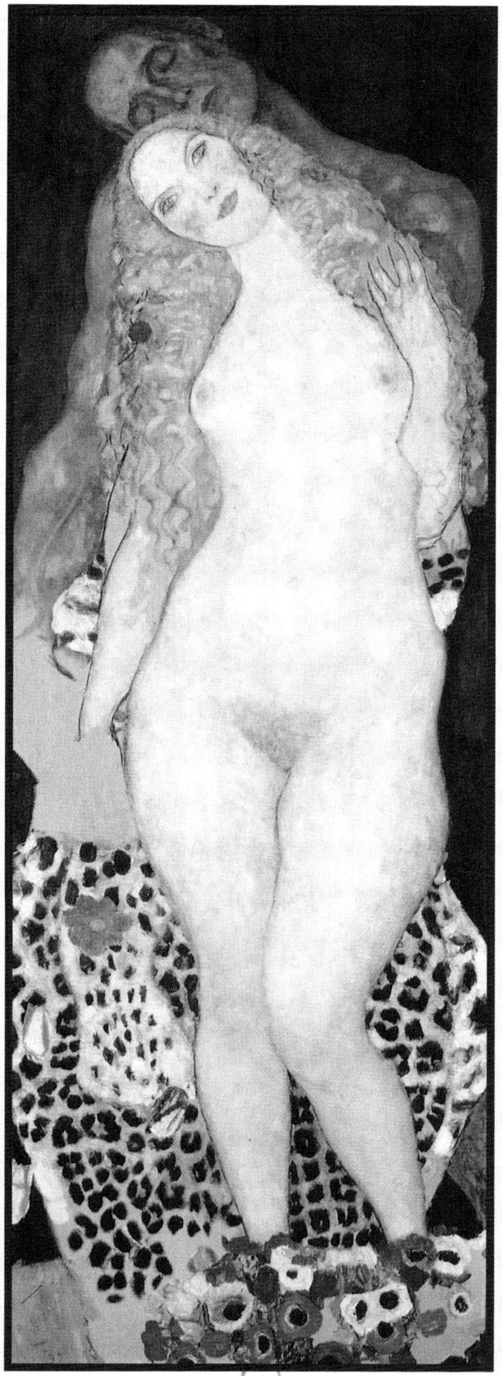

If a culture has created and generally recognizes a symbolic figure standing for all that is womanly, beautiful and desirable, then an artist, in giving physical shape to that idealization, will be at the same time giving physical shape to his abstract conceptualization of Beauty—influenced of course by the preferences, explicit and otherwise, of the period and place where he lives. In a portrait of an actual woman, an artist must incorporate her features into his representation, and therefore must almost necessarily deviate from his mental ideal. But in painting Venus, or Aphrodite, the classical goddess of love and beauty (and therefore, since the time of the Greeks, the symbol of all that is lovely and desirable in a woman), he can give his own, purely abstract ideal physical reality. Then by looking at how Venus/Aphrodite has been depicted over the centuries, we will get a sense of what has been considered the ideal of feminine pulchritude: what remains constant, and what changes in time, according to changes in people's tastes.

Robin Tolmach Lakoff and Raquel L. Scherr from ***Face Value****, 1984*

...a cornucopia of vegetable abundance.

Kenneth Clark describing Rubens' Venus

As the goddess of love Venus can be expected to be richly endowed with secondary sexual characteristics, and usually she is so portrayed. Though exceptions do occur she is more likely to be full of figure than any other frequent female subject of painting. Venus is full as a ripe fruit is full, as a new flower is full, as a swollen stream or budding tree, because she is the symbol of the desire which is at the core of life's ongoingness.

VENUS

Venus...is a nymph of excellent comeliness, born of Heaven and more than others beloved by God on high. Her soul and mind are Love and Charity, her eyes Dignity and Magnanimity, her hands Liberality and Magnificence, her feet Comeliness and Modesty. The whole, then, is Temperance and Honesty, Charm and Splendor. Oh, what exquisite beauty!

Marsilio Ficino

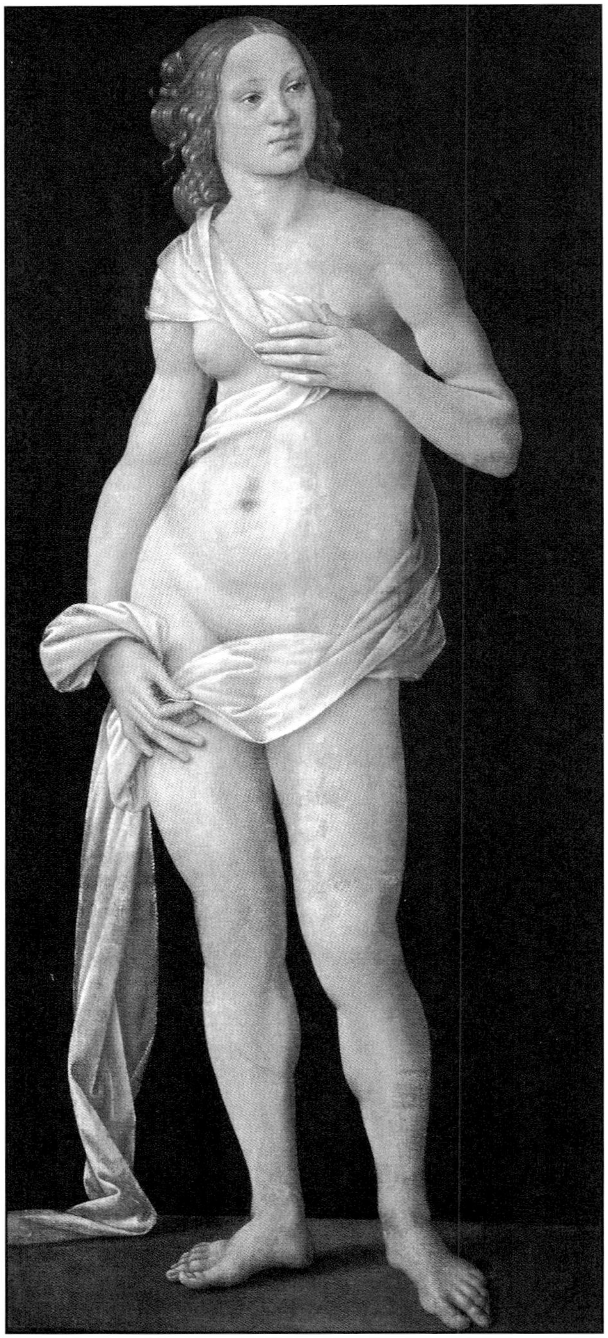

For the ancients...love was symbolized by a goddess whose name meant both beauty and pleasure [Venus]...The body was everything.

*Gabriel Prevost from **Le Nu**, 1883*

The gods and goddesses of the ancient world were visualized and have been traditionally portrayed, as humans of exceptional beauty and grandeur. The fact that so many of them are, by our standards, richly voluptuous reflects the admiration that the artists had for women so formed; it is testimony to how various artists and cultures have conceived feminine beauty.

The graces were, in Greek mythology, three lovely sisters who together represented ideal beauty. Their names translate as Verdure, Goodness and Splendor, and they are frequently, as here, pictured with suitably generous proportions.

Divinities, of either sex, are conceived by our limited imaginations as ideal human beings. Goddesses are ultimately beautiful women, as gods are irresistibly handsome. The fact that so many artistic representations of goddesses shows them to be richly proportioned is further testimony to how artists and cultures have conceived a feminine ideal.

One of the fairest goddesses was Flora, the Roman goddess of flowers and springtime, who married Zephyrus, the gentle god of the south wind, and wandered the earth with him lavishing growth and beauty wherever they went.

She was of perfect classic beauty, divinely tall, and divinely fair, magnificently serene in her movements, big-browed, gentle-eyed, with round arms and fully modulated curves of breasts, and belly.... She was very grand, and as big, I swear it, as the ladies of the Erechtheum. I wished to worship at her shrine.

Morton Fuller, diary entry, 1894

Because your curves and contours are as perfect as a goddess.

Goddess Bra Company tag for generously endowed women's bras.

We remember best what we can see, and thus humankind is continually giving form to abstract entities. The pleasantest form, for most of us, is woman, and thus she bears most of the burden of symbolic personification.

Nations and states can be seen as defined shapes on a map, but these shapes fail to inspire allegiance or enthusiasm. Again woman seems the most useful form, and because our countries are so various, so filled with scenic beauties and natural resources the women chosen to represent them tend towards generous proportions.

To lure, to delight, to appetize, to please, these confer the power to persuade: as the spur to desire, as the excitement of the senses, as a weapon of delight, the female appears down the years to convince us of the messages she conveys.

Marina Warner
from ***Monuments & Maidens****, 1985*

Despite the very real spiritual claims of modesty and simplicity most of us see the good life as one of profusion. We admire the spare wisdom of the monastic life, but most of us, when asked to choose, select the full laden and splendidly furnished palace. Perhaps the promise land is barren, but most of us envision its fruit laden trees, its flower filled gardens, its many rivers and lakes. So, when challenged to see Canada or Illinois as a woman, one is likely to see her as voluptuously endowed and richly appareled.

When artists, confronted with a blank canvas, reach down into themselves for a way to picture an abstraction they are first inclined to give it human form, then select female form, next try to make it suitable to the concept involved, and finally they try to make the forms pleasing.

In the symbol, the particular represents the general, ***not*** *as a dream,* ***not*** *as a shadow, but as a living and momentary revelation of the inscrutable.*

J.W. von Goethe from ***Collected Essays****, 1817*

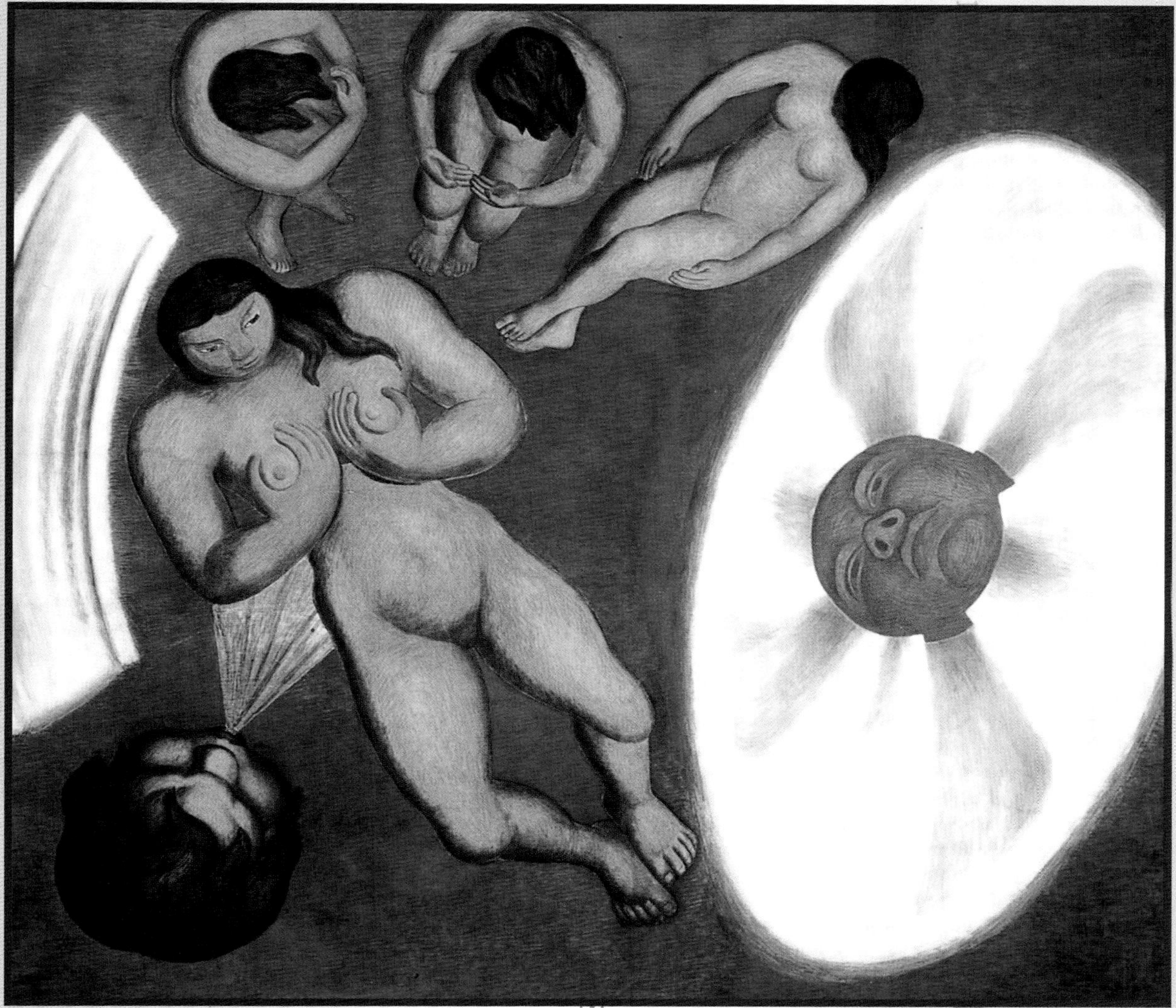

Abundance is a wonderful concept. *The Oxford English Dictionary* defines it as an: "overflowing state or condition...enough and more that enough—plentifulness, copiousness." In a world in which too little is frequently the portion the mere word abundance makes me smile.

In those days, the contours of Ceres were more fashionable than those of Venus, and my mother's ripe curves were much admired. To conform to such standards, handkerchiefs padded out some of the bodices of her flatter-chested friends.

Sonia Keppel from ***Edwardian Daughter****, 1958*

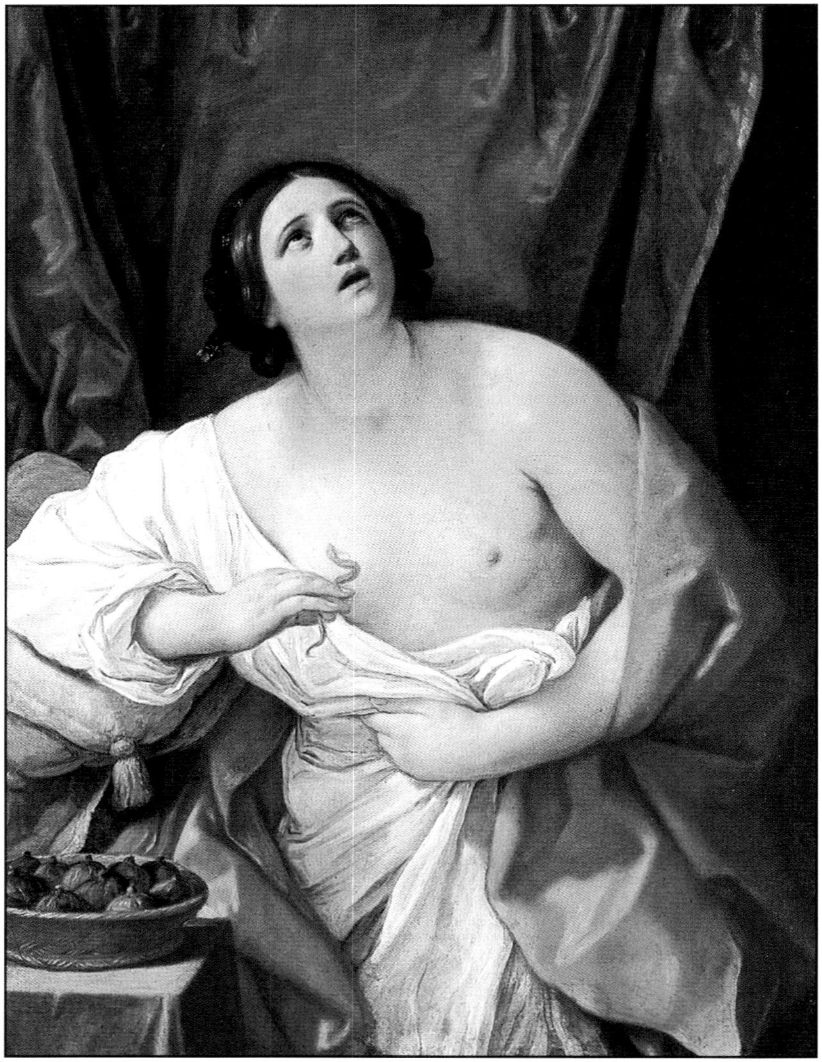

We step down from goddesses to symbolic representations to heroines— fully human, but magnificently so.

Cleopatra, whatever her real appearance, became a legend as an irresistible beauty. She entranced Marc Anthony, and then Julius Caesar, who, according to the Roman author Lucan, gave her the crown of Egypt because "her face supported her petition and her wicked beauty gained her suit." Each age makes Cleopatra beautiful after its own fashion, and each artist according to their own taste.

CLEOPATRA

The beauty of Bathsheba was so great that King David was immediately filled with desire, and he immediately acted out that desire. One might imagine that David was frequently so inspired, but the biblical chronicler, who spares him not at all in this, or other situations, does not report similar episodes.

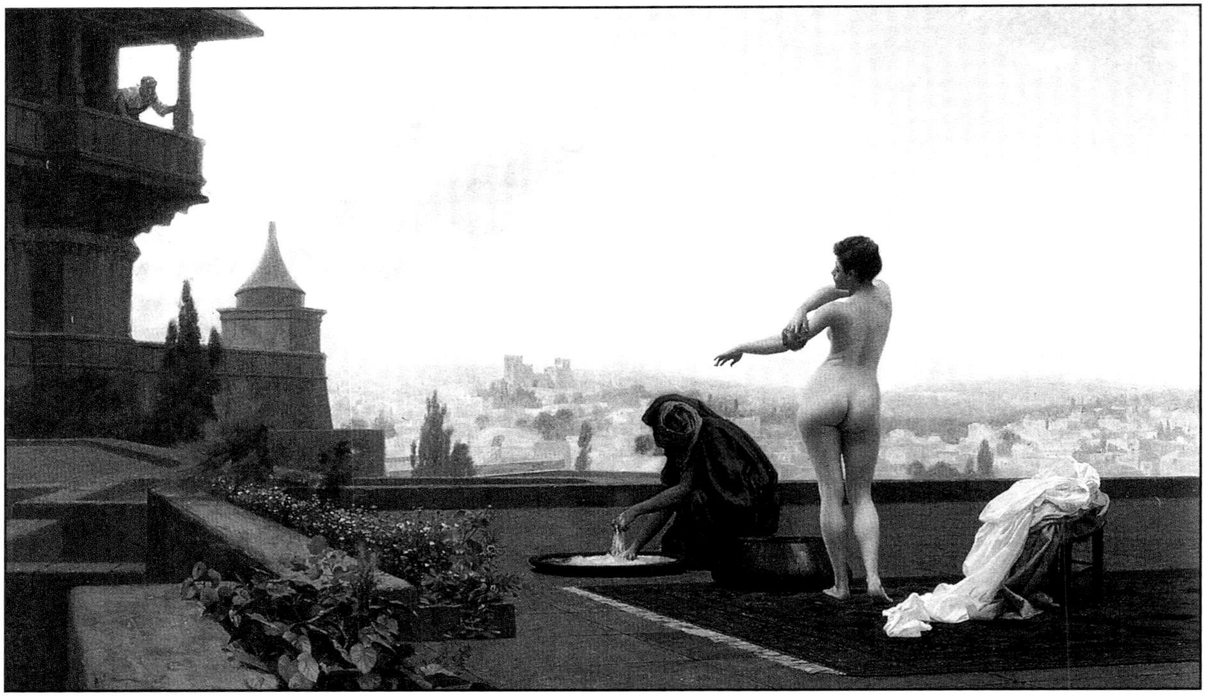

It happened, late one afternoon, when David arose from his couch and was walking upon the roof of the king's house, that he saw from the roof a woman bathing; and the woman was very beautiful. And David sent and inquired about the woman. And one said, "Is not this Bathshe'ba, the daughter of Eli'am, the wife of Uri'ah the Hittite?" So David sent messengers and took her; and she came to him, and he lay with her.

2 Samuel 11

BATHSHEBA

Hilda has appeared on Brown and Bigelow calendars for 43 consecutive years, and is still going strong on a 1999 calendar. Brown and Bigelow of St. Paul, Minnesota, is the world's largest calendar producer. They were founded in 1898, and sell advertising calendars around the world. Among their most popular calendars have been western scenes by Charles M. Russell, poker playing dogs by C.M. Coolidge, and Norman Rockwell's Boy Scout calendars. Duane Bryer's Hilda calendars have lasted longer than any of these, testimony to the lasting appeal of voluptuous young women.

The well-rounded Hilda, appearing in various stages of dishabille, is loved by women, according to Bryers, because "she glorifies plump girls," Asked if one of Hilda's pet poses was inspired by the immortal "September Morn," the artist chuckles and answers, "She developed from my carnal mind."

Allen Scott

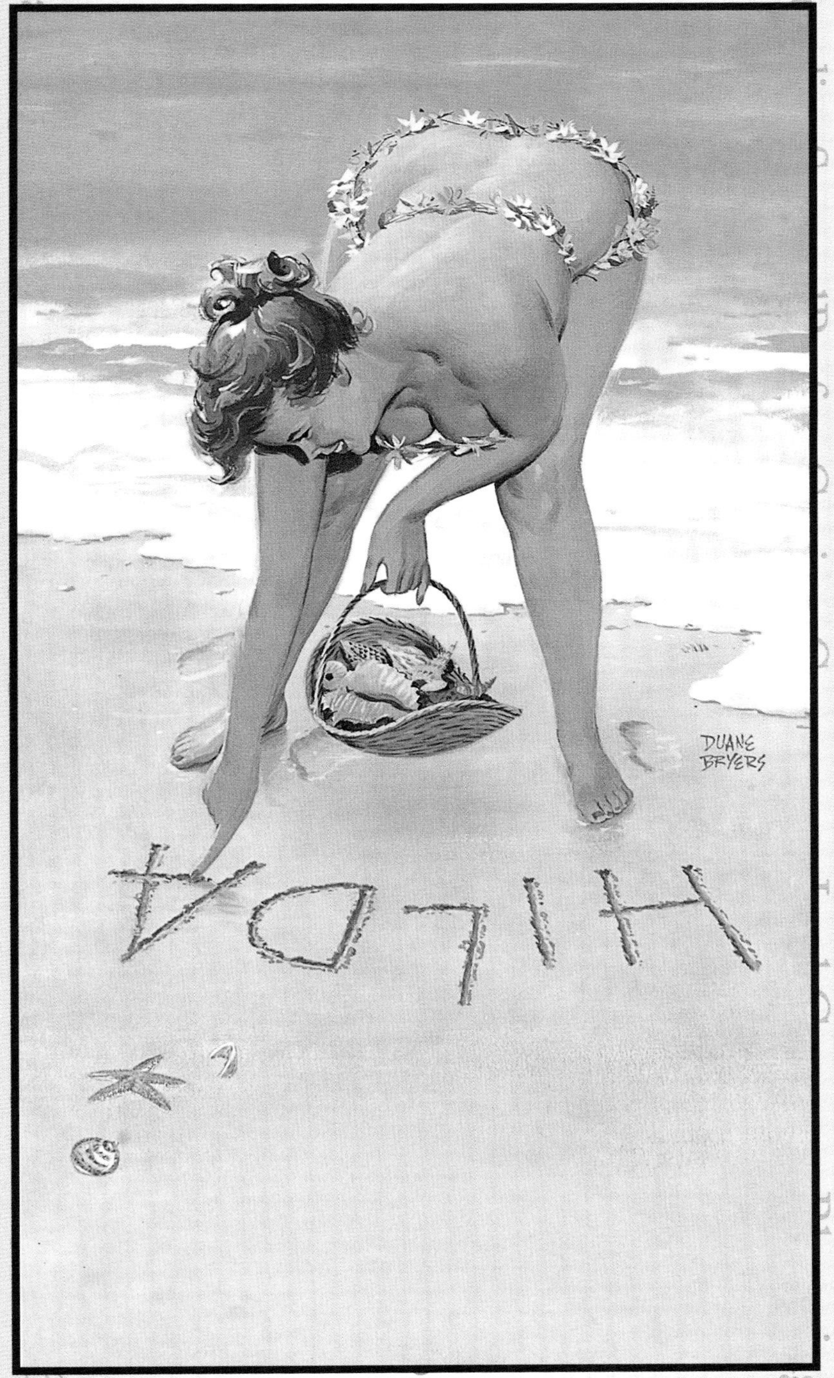
DUANE BRYERS
HILDA

Hilda's popularity has been so sustained not merely because she is curvaceous and scantily clad, but also because of the character and demeanor that develop through the pictures. She is always seen humorously. We enjoy her uninhibitedly because she is herself acting without inhibition. She is never trying to be alluring, in fact she is unaware that we are watching. She is coming out of her garments not because she has dressed to be provocative, but rather because she had dressed carelessly and with materials at hand, and because her many curves are difficult to conceal. Hilda is simply a woman who energetically enjoys her daily life. She never poses. A naturally opulent figure seems just right for this naturally unpretentious young woman.

HILDA

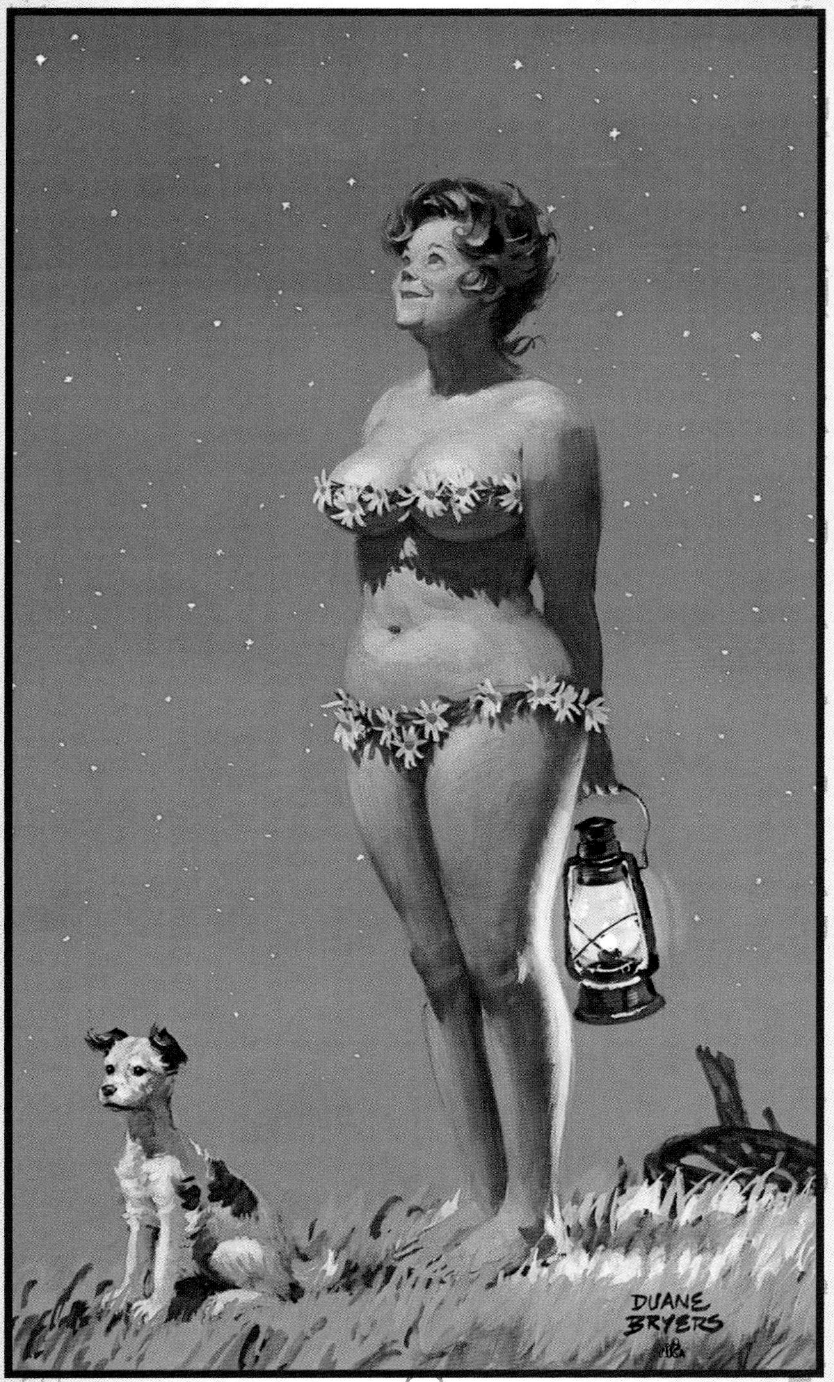

It is difficult to pinpoint Rembrandt's ideal of womanly beauty. He painted with great enthusiasm the women he loved, but also seemed to achieve a sympathetic identification with whoever he painted that bordered on love. Old or young, man or woman, well nourished or starving, well-kempt or ragged—he loved them all, treasuring each for what they were. Like Chaucer he delighted in the possession of personality, and found ways to make us see and feel as he did. One thing is clear about his view of woman and beauty—an abundance of flesh in no way disqualified a woman from a profound attractiveness.

...when Rembrandt depicts the emotion shining through Bathsheba's face as she ponders over King David's letter he achieves a kind of beauty which is dependent on inner life and not on physical form.

Kenneth Clark from ***Feminine Beauty****, 1980*

If he [Rembrandt] painted, as sometimes would happen, a nude woman, he chose no Greek Venus as his model, but rather a washerwoman or a treader of peat from a barn…

Andries Pels from ***Use and Misuse of the Theater****, 1932*

In these common Dutch women he found the elemental beauty and dignity which all women share beneath their surface differences.

Andrew Foster, 1932

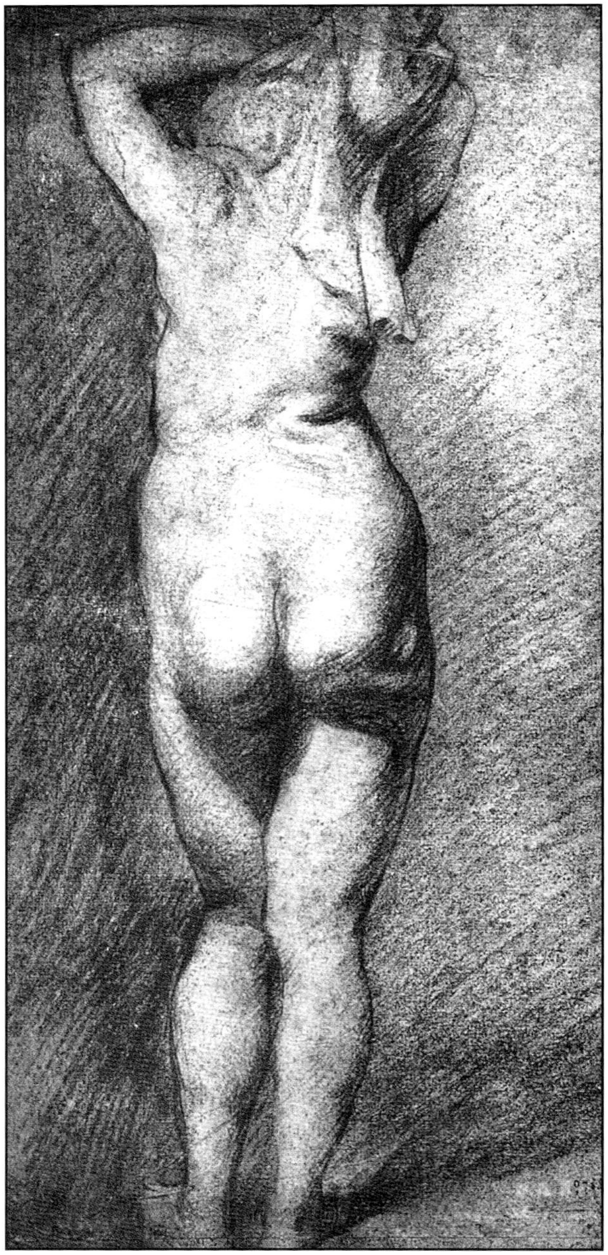

No other painter in his personality, thought and art is more typical of the Baroque Age than Pieter Paul Rubens, its great exponent. Woman and the beauty of her body were his primary preoccupation. But how far removed are his women from the ideals of the Renaissance! As they appear, as Venus at her Toilet, Susanna in the Bath, as Angelica with the Hermits, as Graces or as Mortals in the Garden of Love, they are invariably sensual representations of an exaggerated super-dimensional femininity. The body has become a mountain of flesh, soft, full of warm genuine life, the forms curving in more and more unbridled joy in their own nature. But this is not only a beautiful lustless existence as it was in Renaissance painting until Correggio, but an aware existence, a feast of sensuality.

Bodo Cichy from ***Masterpieces of Figure Painting****, 1959*

PIETER PAUL RUBENS

Glory to that Homer of painting [Rubens], to that father of warmth and enthusiasm.

Eugène Delacroix, journal entry, 1853

But in the end the greatness of Rubens does not lie in the realm of technique, but in that of imagination. He takes the female body, the plump, comfortable, clothed female body of the North, and transforms it imaginatively with less sacrifice of its carnal reality than had ever been necessary before. He creates a new, complete race of women.

Kenneth Clark from ***The Nude****, 1956*

PIETER PAUL RUBENS

Rubens…was the greatest religious painter of his time, and in his splendidly unified character sensuality could not be dissociated from praise.

We thank Thee then, O Father,
For all things bright and good,
The seedtime and the harvest,
Our life, our health, our food:
Accept the gifts we offer….

As we sing these words on a bright Sunday in September we may approach for a minute the spirit in which Rubens painted his pictures. The golden hair and swelling bosoms of his Graces are hymns of thanksgiving for abundance, and they are placed before us with the same unself-conscious piety as the sheaves of corn and piled-up pumpkins that decorate a village church at harvest festival.

Kenneth Clark from ***The Nude****, 1956*

…it was Rubens who inspired both Watteau and Boucher. He was a master of the baroque, and the bottom is a baroque form, harmonizing with the clouds and garlands of late-baroque decoration.

Kenneth Clark from ***The Nude****, 1956*

PIETER PAUL RUBENS

Renoir painted, from first to last, subjects which made him feel good, and which he hoped would do the same for viewers. He liked babies, and picnics, flowers, people in nice clothes, and the shadows made by trees on sunny days, spring and summer—but most of all he liked buxom women, unashamed of their beauty and in full possession of health and youth. Winter and old age, gloom and grayness did not interest him. Compare his palette to Cezanne's; compare his subjects to Van Gogh. The dark side, even the shadowed side, has no appeal to him. As he grew old the vision did not weaken, it intensified. His women, who have always been glowing and curvaceous, now are sensual amazons, so large and strong and lovely that they seem to be goddesses rather than mere mortals.

Renoir goes back to the source, to the delightful, carnal eighteenth century, cultured but ardent, with its pleasant, melancholic, gentle, and voluptuous human nature.

André Derain

PIERRE—AUGUSTE RENOIR

For it is indeed love of the body we discover finally in the paintings of Renoir. These women are fecund, fertile, nubile, ripe, pregnant, abundant, ebullient, teeming, swelling.

Kim Chernin from **The Obsession**, *1981*

PIERRE—AUGUSTE RENOIR

Instinctively we know that this affirmative vision requires the women this painter uses for his models to be as large as possible, so that the sheer magnitude of life's richness can be embodied in an expressive and representational form. Thus, the women in a Renoir canvas are huge; by our standards they are fat and they become, with their voluptuous abundance, portraits of life ***(la vie)****, dancing, bathing, forever in motion, life contemplative along the riverside, and one is drawn towards them through a force that is larger than the sexual, drawn down into this feminine side of existence, with its rounded forms and dappled surfaces, its rose tints and hues, which seem to stand for sensuality itself.*

Kim Chernin from ***The Obsession****, 1981*

PIERRE—AUGUSTE RENOIR

All the plump girls whom he [Renoir] painted on green banks under trees, their fat so permeated by light that they seem like luminous flowers; yet they are flesh, and full-bloodied flesh that would bleed.

George Moore from ***Vale****, 1914*

In these years we watch Renoir gradually abandoning the fair, round girls who had won him popularity and creating a new race of women, massive, ruddy, unseductive, but with the weight and unity of great sculpture.

Kenneth Clark from ***The Nude****, 1956*

PIERRE—AUGUSTE RENOIR

Kustodiev was an enormously popular painter whose career spanned the end of the Czarist era and the early years of the Soviet state. His most characteristic work lies in his portraits of provincial merchants' wives. (All of the paintings reproduced here are such pictures, expect for the sailor and girl on page 86, which is from a series he called "Russian Types.") He saw these women as spoiled, vain, overfed creatures, and to some extent the portraits are satirical, but his admiration for their fleshy splendor could not be concealed. Further, he makes it clear that this was the kind of woman that was admired in provincial Russia, and despite his laughter, they do emerge as gorgeous beings.

A remarkable fact about Kustodiev is that, while still young, he was struck with a crippling illness that kept him immobile and suffering for the rest of his life. All of the paintings here reproduced were created under these conditions, and it is easy to speculate that one so shattered in body should enjoy bodies so vibrant with life.

BORIS KUSTODIEV

[Kustodiev] employed all his expressive means to fulfill this objective, to create an image of Rus, of provincial Russia, personified in folk poetry as the fair maid.

Victoria Lebedeva from ***Boris Kustodiev and His Work****, 1981*

The ***Merchant Wife*** *theme gave the artist a medium for the exaltation and poetisation of the provinces. For all their conventionality his pictures are still striking epitomes of patriarchal Russia with its corpulent beauties, golden cupolas and wide-open spaces. The viewer is overcome by a feeling of confusion as he gazes at this complacent realm of flesh in excelsis, a feeling which does not come straightaway but only as he meditates on the inner essence of the pictures.*

Victoria Lebedeva
from ***Boris Kustodiev and His Work****, 1981*

РУССКАЯ
ВЕНЕРА

The artist admires the people who live in this garish, barbaric world. He delights in their beauty, the beauty of sleek animals, with a natural awareness of their own perfection.

Victoria Lebedeva from ***Boris Kustodiev and His Work****, 1981*

BORIS KUSTODIEV

Maillol was an artist with one subject—the female nude. Only one kind of woman appealed to him—heavy and curvaceous. When she was young his wife was his only model. When she grew old he found models who resembled her when young. He did not seek variety. For him the form of woman was the only truth he sought; the pursuit of beauty lay only in homage to her.

...Maillol's work sought to capture a beauty that expressed, rather than an idealization of the human body, ...a sensation of the body in all its immediacy as a thing that is beautiful in itself and not as an idealization of beauty...

Bertrand Lorquin from ***Maillol***

ARISTIDE MAILLOL

My wife is the goddess I am searching to express in all things.

Gaston Lachaise

...the indomitable pagan [Lachaise] who saw the entire universe in the form of a woman.

Marsden Hartley

Lachaise did not work from nature because he had a powerful vision that has haunted men since time immemorial of a voluptuous mother goddess who is neither madonna nor whore, but an abundant, generous, fertility and creation symbol.

Barbara Rose from ***Gaston Lachaise Sculpture****, 1991*

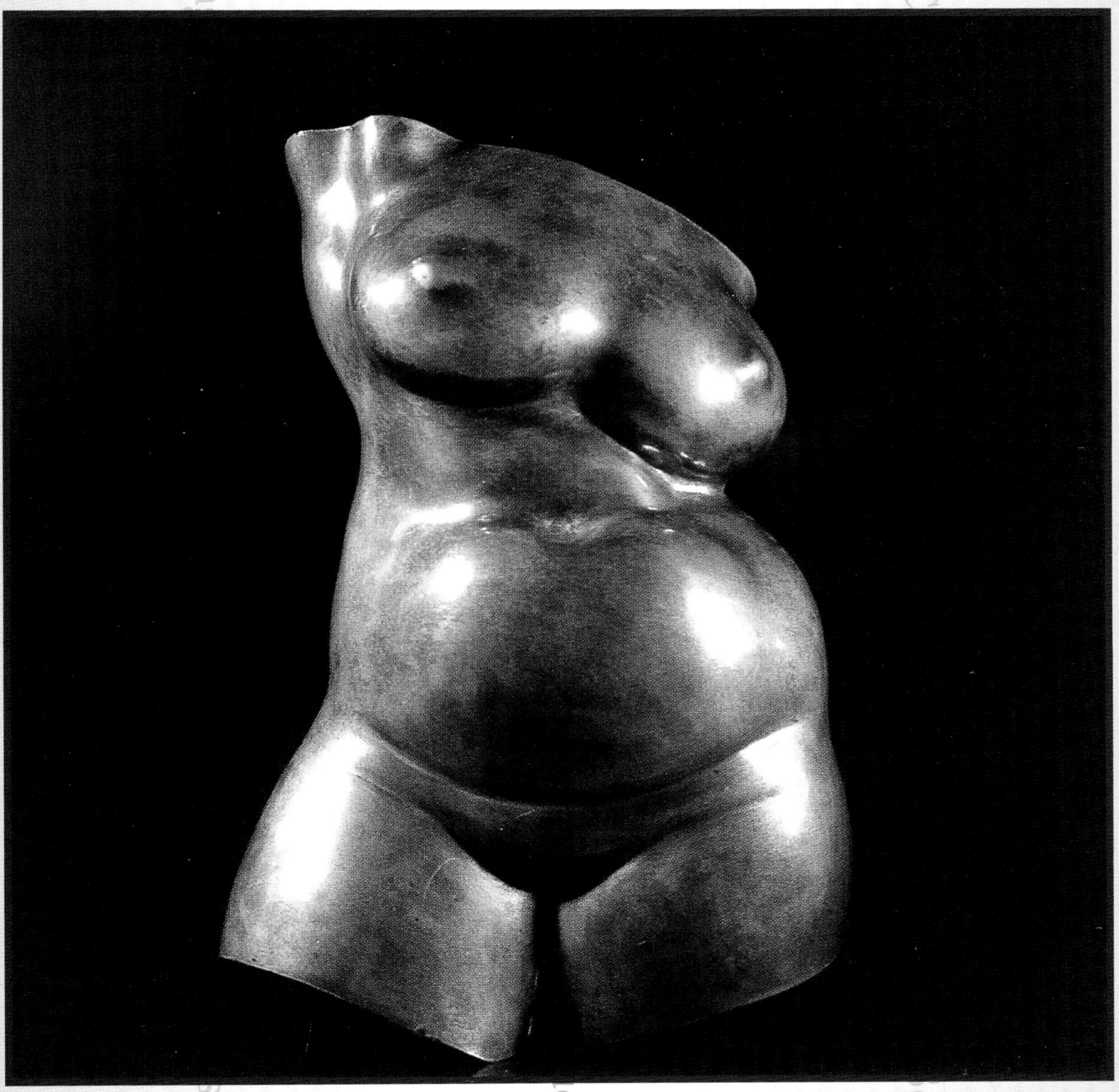

Reginald Marsh embraced New York City, and made of it his life work. He loved the teeming streets, the crowded shops, the prize fights, Coney Island beach, the burlesque theaters—wherever the people assembled in large numbers, and gave themselves up to the passion of living. Many of his women were richly formed because these were the women he most enjoyed, the ones who embraced life with the greatest enthusiasm.

A woman, for him, he once said, "is always a stimulus to paint." Nowhere is this image of woman—ideal, remote, aloof, yet buxom and alluring—more clear than in his recurrent theme, the woman on the merry-go-round horse.

Marilyn Cohen from ***Reginald Marsh's New York****, 1983*

REGINALD MARSH 44

Picasso, unlike a realist such as Marsh, paid little attention to the details of reality. The women he pictured were not women seen on the streets, but the women he found deep in his own consciousness. One of his wives once said: "If my husband met a woman on the street who looked like the women in his paintings he would collapse in a dead faint." Why then are so many of them heavy, monumental? I believe it is because he sought the essence of woman, and felt the essence to lie in curves and substance.

...the artist who does not limit his sympathies to the fashionably disembodied female, sides with the primitive, and celebrates massive womanhood.

Bernard Rudofsky from ***The Unfashionable Human Body****, 1971*

Picasso
1905 Schoorl

Various explanations for Picasso's current obsession with gigantic, swollen human forms have been given—Olga's pregnancy in 1920–21, and recurrent dreams he had had as a child in which limbs swelled and retracted irrationally and frighteningly. But the works of art he had recently been looking at may be a more significant factor. For instance, it is hard not to believe that this wonderful painting was not directly inspired by the massive headless figures of the 'Three Fates' from the east pediment of the Parthenon (in particular the upright figure), or by the huge statue of Demeter from Cnidos: the unusually crisp folds of the drapery in the painting imitate the drapery of these sculptures. (Picasso had spent three months in London in 1919 while he was working on his designs for the ballet **Le Tricorne** *and would have seen all these figures in the British Museum.) The sense of massive size and cumbrous weight is equally potent in some of the greatest frescoes from Herculaneum and Pompeii (such as the 'Herakles and Telephus' in the Archaeological Museum in Naples, and the great cycle in the Villa of the Mysteries, Pompeii), for in these the brightly lit life-sized bodies of the women push out from flat backgrounds. Picasso must also have been impressed by similar effects in the great fresco cycles of Michelangelo and Annibale Carracci that he saw in Rome.*

Elizabeth Cowling and Jennifer Mundy from ***On Classic Ground**, 1990*

The physical ideal at the turn of the century was the woman with "fascinating and beautiful curves." The "fine figure" was "perfectly free from all scrawny and hollow places," with "a bust as full, plump, and firm as you could desire." Lucille recalled that her fashion models were "six foot one of perfect symmetry" and "statuesque": "No one of them weighed under eleven stone, and several of them weighed considerably more. They were 'big girls' with 'fine figures'...It was the day of tall women with gracious curves." The thin woman was given short shrift and was rudely told to "cover some of her angles." If anything, the Edwardian beauty was taller, weighed more, and had a larger bosom than her predecessor

Valerie Steele from ***Fashion and Eroticism****, 1985*

In the mid-nineteenth century, hotels and bars were adorned with Bouguereau-inspired paintings of voluptuous female nudes; Lillian Russell, the most photographed woman in America in 1890, was known and admired for her hearty appetite, ample body (over two hundred pounds at the height of her popularity), and "challenging, fleshly arresting" beauty.

Susan Bordo from ***Unbearable Weight****, 1993*

Between the 1860s and the 1880s, rotundity gained ground for men as well as women. European dress styles emphasized the "semblance of embonpoint," as a British observer noted among women in Boston in 1859. Portrait painters stressed buxom qualities. Doctors urged the importance of solid weight in their growing campaign against nervousness. S. Weir Mitchell demonstrated how skinny forms correlated with discontented, nervous personalities. Actresses at all levels of the stage illustrated and promoted fashionable plumpness, adding bustles to a corseting designed to stress ample bosoms and derrieres. Costume, indeed, intended rather to rearrange fat than minimize it, while newspaper advertisements featured nostrums designed to help weight gain long before their columns opened up to diet products.

Peter N. Stearns from ***Fat History****, 1997*

2ME. EXPOSITION
NATIONALE SUISSE
DE L'AUTOMOBILE
ET DU CYCLE
1906
GENÈVE
28 Avril – 6 Mai
1906
PIK
KUNSTANSTALT MÜLLER & ZÜRICH

"La jeune fille is a lady the chief defect of whose figure is the lack of it!...The general run of girls suffer from a paucity of curves and contours." Girls tended to have "scraggy" figures and "callow shoulders—I am being truthful but unkind!" The author described one dress that, in her opinion, would have been "a charming gown for a woman of thirty!...It was exceedingly pretty, but it would have wanted the shoulders of a woman of the world, if you know what I mean...not the probably too visible collar-bone and shoulder-blades of a child of seventeen!"

Mrs. Nepean from ***The Queen****, 1903 as quoted by Valerie Steele in* ***Fashion and Eroticism***

THE GREAT CAPADURA
HAS BEEN, IS NOW, AND EVER SHALL BE
THE BEST 5 Ct. CIGAR IN THE WORLD.

Miss Russell was worth it. We muzhiks didn't see very much of her, but what we did see was ravishing. Maybe her waist wasn't so small as some of the others, but it looked even smaller, her hips were so gorgeous and stately and her broad, white bosom so ample. She threw back her golden head and caroled coquettishly when her hero made love to her, she caroled severely at the villain, and she danced till the old Hype stage shook.

Clarence Day describing an encounter with Lillian Russell [Lillian Russell in 1899 had a 42-inch bust and weighed 186 pounds.]

It is very nice to see a woman round and plump, but when the plumpness becomes positive obesity, then it is no longer a beauty. Extreme thinness is a much more cruel enemy to beauty than extreme stoutness.

A Professional Beauty from ***Beauty and How to Keep It****, 1889*

OPERA DIVAS

Opera stars are frequently large people. Particularly in the old days before amplification, they needed to fill opera houses with their voices. Large chests hold more breath than small ones, and large chests are usually a part of large bodies. Further, people tend to grow larger as they grow older, and singers ordinarily achieve stardom in their middle years. Thus, divas tend to size. Opera fans, however, do not merely tolerate the large women who sing—they celebrate their size, joy in their majestic presence. The nature of opera includes exaggerated and highly dramatic action; large singers seem right for such moods and events.

Singers are supposedly fat. The body must be huge. The body must spill over, embarrass itself, declare immensity.

Wayne Koestenbaum from ***The Queen's Throat****, 1993*

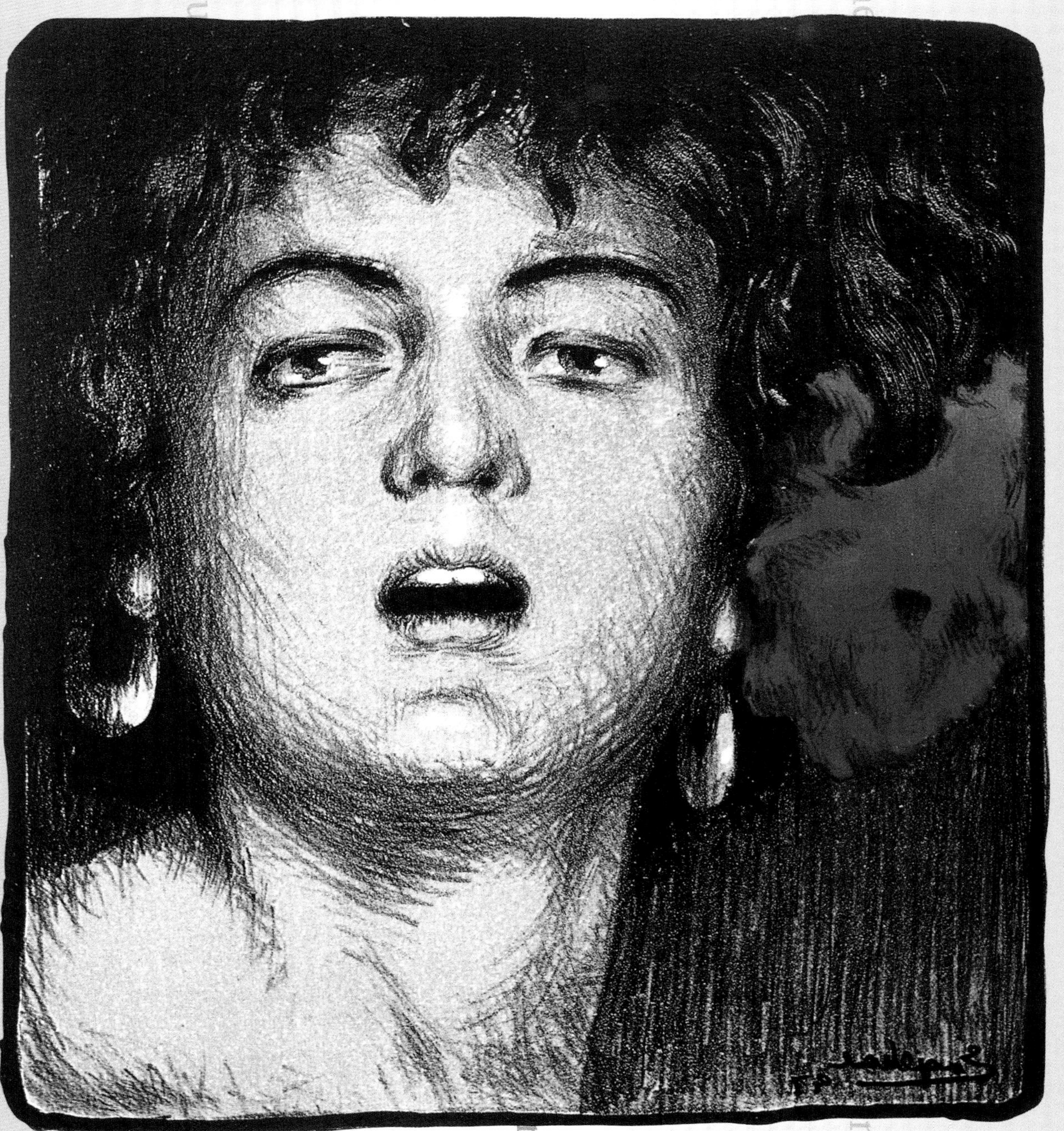

I go to the opera house because I love the splendid sets, the masses of people in antique costume, the huge orchestra blaring beneath the stage, the instant loves and renunciations, the flashing swords and cups raised in mass toasts, the singers sweating and singing at the top of their voices—but most of all I go for the shapely giantesses who bloom on its stage like massive tropical flowers.

Edward Hoagland, 1970

© MISHKIN NY

In the nineteenth century models of female beauty were not as available as they are today, and so women of the theater were of great importance, because it was a place where scantily clad women were available for viewing. Starting in 1869, and continuing to the end of the century, a vaudeville troupe called The British Blondes toured the United Sates. The girls selected for these tours had remarkable voluptuous figures, and they were enormously popular. The producer later recalled, " the entire male citizenry of your republic threw open their arms to us in a welcoming embrace." A contemporary chronicler said they had, to a remarkable degree, "curves, undulations and sinuosity." Whether the British Blondes were the result of a groundswell of enthusiasm for richly endowed women, or whether they helped to create one, we cannot know, but their tours parallel the flowering of a taste for voluptuous women, and the theater was frequently their showcase. This tendency was dominant through the 1890's, and then was challenged by a variety of other models, but buxom women were a frequent attraction on the stage until a craze for thinness in the 1920s made them rarities.

SCALA
REVUE À POIVRE
8 TABLEAUX DE E.P. LAFARGUE

Every period has its own ideal image of female beauty. At the turn of the century ample, voluptuous female figures were all the rage. The sedate bourgeois succumbed all too easily to the attractions of the ***femme fatale.*** *In the reviews, the entertainment halls, the cabarets, and the variety theaters of Paris, an unending procession of sumptuous daughters of Venus made its way across the stage night after night. Grün mastered the art of presenting these scarlet-clad, veiled Bacchantes, who flung themselves wholeheartedly and ecstatically into the glare of the footlights long before the barren routine of professional striptease was to come.*

Hermann Schardt from ***Paris 1900****, 1970*

Bathing costumes have always revealed more of a woman's figure than everyday dress, and thus the fashionable shape of each era is most strikingly revealed on the beach. Further, there is a tendency toward fullness, for even women who are content with themselves may feel awkward about appearing in a bathing suit if they do not fill it out adequately.

THE WINNING POST
SUMMER
ANNUAL
1907
Edited by
R.S. Sievier
Illustrated by
The Snark
ONE SHILLING NETT

We expect young animals to be plump. Babies are patterns of concentric circles. Kittens and puppies are round and cute. The young, of all species, tend to have a protective layer of fat. Females tend to keep this fat as they ripen into maturity, and plumpness charms us as youthful potentiality always charms.

During youth…woman is farther distinguished by the softness, the smoothness, the delicacy, and the polish, of all the forms, by the gradual and east transition between all the parts, by the number and the harmony of the undulating lines which these present in every view, by the beautiful outline of the reliefs, and by the fineness and the animation of the skin.

Alexander Walker from ***Beauty****, 1843*

Motherhood is inextricably tied to fullness. Pregnancy causes enlargement. Lactation causes larger breasts. The mood of mothering is one of bountiful expansion.

What baby ever wished that his mother was slimmer,
her hips narrower, her breasts less full?

Sydney Smith, 1917

Recently, many books and articles have been written decrying the craze for thinness, and the resultant shame engendered in women who are, in fact, normally shaped. Most of them urge women to accept themselves as they are, rejecting the standards imposed by fashion magazines and other false prophets. Others stress that men have, from earliest times, imposed on women there own capricious ideas of feminine beauty. I do not disagree with these emphases, but I do want to stress that heavy women are, for many people, superior in attractiveness, and that an awareness of this can secure for such women the confidence and pride which are a central component of beauty.

At no period has a passionate cult of beauty for its own sake been more triumphantly proclaimed than when the great Venetian painters were in their prime. Titian's and Tintoretto's superb portraits of large-limbed women, their golden tresses intertwined with jewels, successfully fuse the ideal with the real. It is the beauty of slow movement, full breasts and vast riches. The luxury of Venice, perhaps the most extreme ever known in Europe, was used to enchant, not obscure their beauty.

Madge Garland from ***The Changing Face of Beauty****, 1957*

...all these admirable characteristics of female form, the mere existence of which in woman must, one is tempted to imagine, be, even to herself, a source of ineffable pleasure—these constitute a being worthy, as the personification of beauty, of occupying the temples of Greece; present an object finer, alas! than nature seems even capable of producing; and offer to all nations and ages a theme of admiration and delight.

Alexander Walker from ***Beauty****, 1843*

After I've been at work. I get undressed, I look in the mirror. I realize it's my own body I've been modeling all day. Rings of flesh, massive plains, mountainous plateaus of flesh. Suddenly, I'm in a glory of fleshy existence. I see power in it, in my own body, fertility, abundance. A large, unrestricted sense of life.

Kim Chernin from ***The Obsession****, 1981*

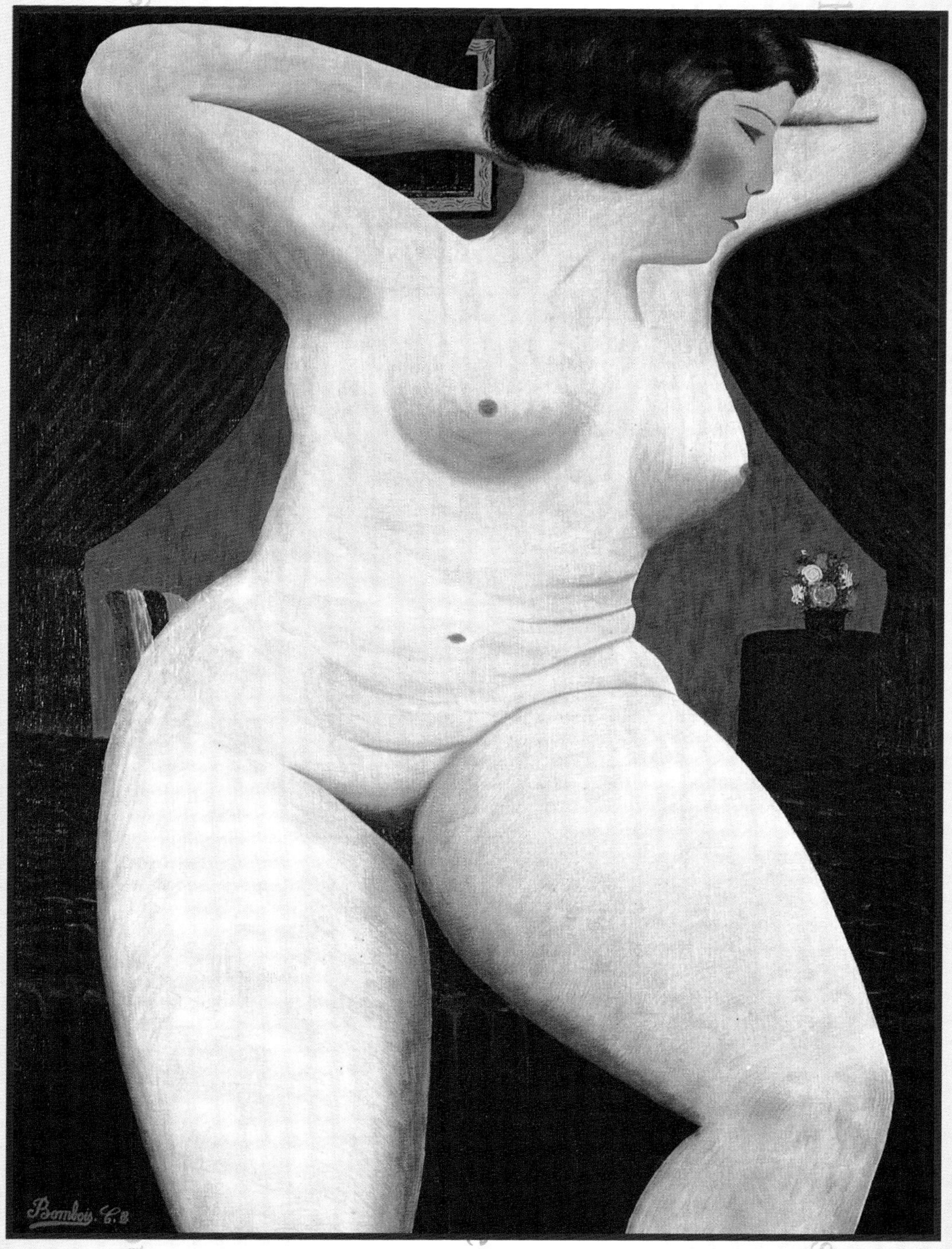

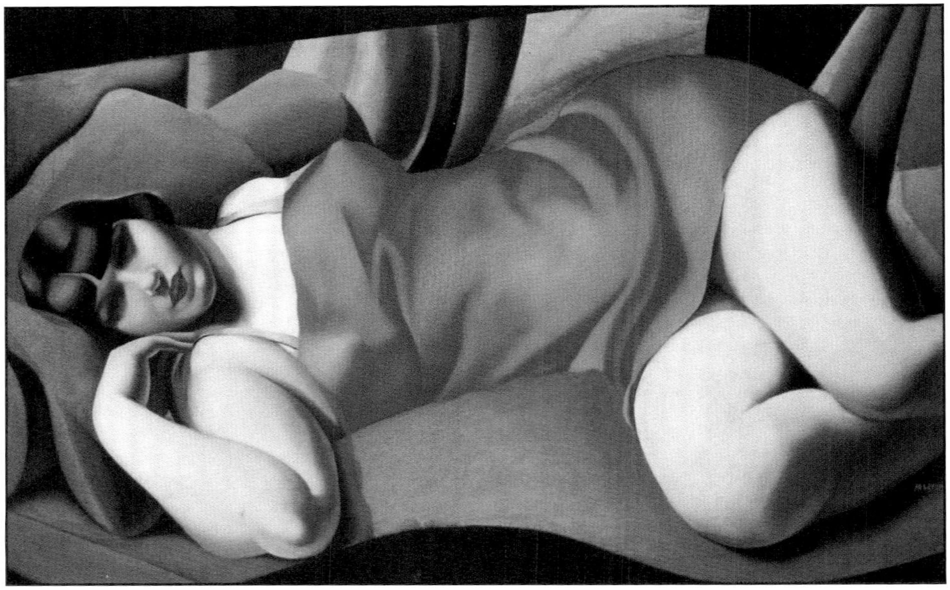

these hips are big hips
they need space to
move around in.
they don't fit into little
pretty places. these hips
are free hips.
they don't like to be held back.
these hips have never been enslaved,
they go where they want to go
they do what they want to do.
these hips are mighty hips.
these hips are magic hips.
I have known them
to put a spell on a man and
spin him like a top!

Lucille Clifton from ***Two-Headed Woman****, 1980*

Metzinger

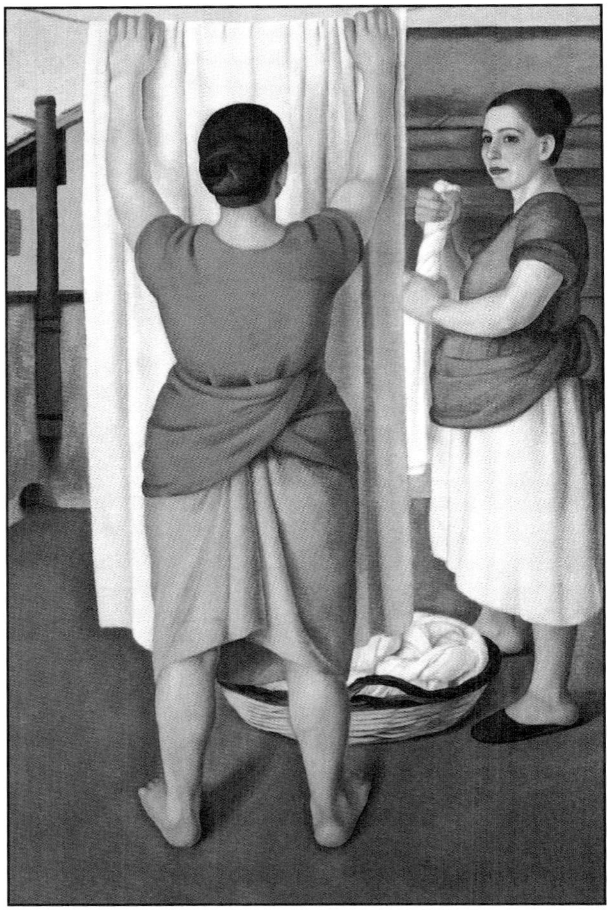

Though it is true that standards of human beauty vary greatly from time to time and place to place, it is also true that certain tendencies emerge in the vast majority of cultures. Symmetrical features are usually those most admired. An emphasis on the natural differences between men and women is usually an underlying criteria, and pronounced breasts and hips are most frequently admired in women. According to ethnographic reports from The Human Relations Area Files: "As far as general body build is concerned, the majority of societies whose preferences in this matter are recorded feel that a plump woman is more attractive than a thin one."

[Ebony Magazine]...urged that black women should reject the "think thin fad" companies, while learning to dress to highlight their best features. Furthermore,...Ebony recurrently noted how much black men appreciated some real heft in a woman. "I've never been attracted to thin or even average-size sisters. I need a woman I can hold on to. Truth be told, my ideal woman is a size 20," reported a graduate of the University of the District of Columbia. "The only thing a thin woman can do for me is introduce me to a woman of size." Men's aesthetic judgments often mirrored those of the woman themselves, in a clearly distinctive subculture concerning body standards.

Peter N. Stearns from ***Fat History****, 1997*

...a strong presumptive case for the general desirability of fat women can be made from the ethnographic evidence: Of a total of twenty-six tribes from all over the inhabited globe who have ever been put on record as expressing any preference in the matter, only five preferred their women slender.

Anne Scott Beller from ***Fat & Thin****, 1997*

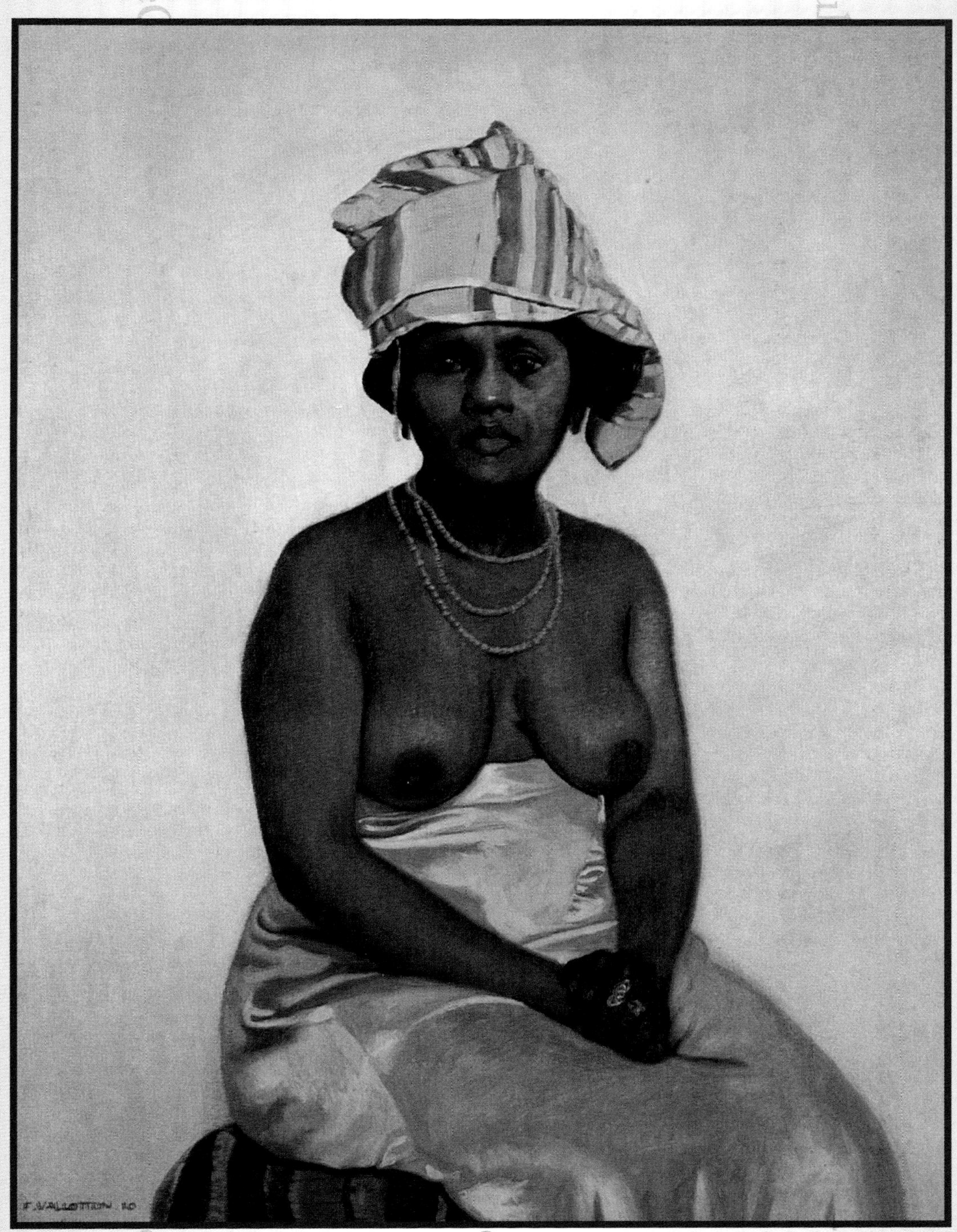
F. VALLOTTON. 10

Her face is pleasing as the full moon. Her body is well clothed with flesh and as soft as the mustard flower. Her skin is fine, tender, and fair as the yellow lotus... Her eyes are bright and beautiful as the orbs of the fawn, well-shaped and with reddish corners. Her bosom is full and high. She has a good neck; her nose is straight and lovely, and three folds or wrinkles cross her middle—above the umbilical region.

Havelock Ellis, describing the Hindu feminine ideal

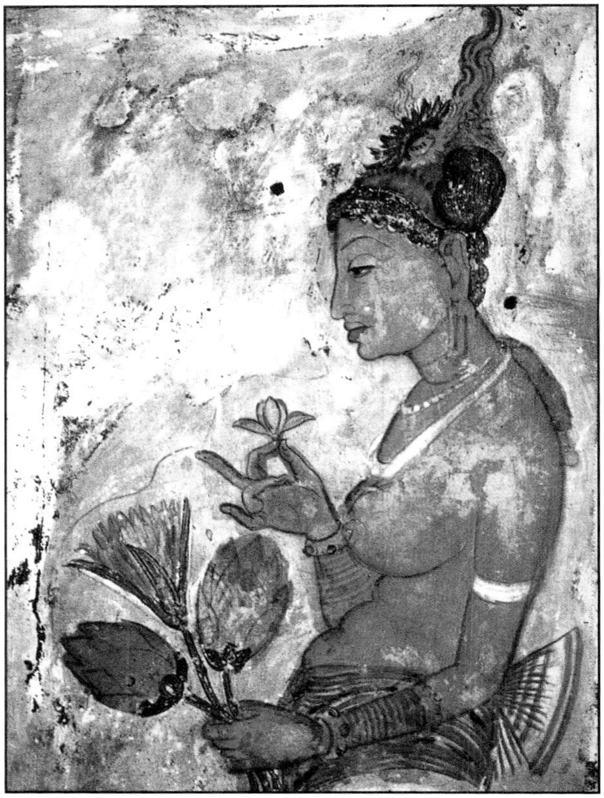

Fatness at its best is associated with moistness, fertility, and ***kindness*** *(a sociable and giving nature) as well as with happiness, vitality, and bodily health in general. People know that drinks and warm, moist, cooked food can fatten them, while cold rice,* ***overnight*** *food (leftovers), and dryers such as store-bought crackers usually cannot. Fatness connotes fullness and juicy ripeness, like that of ripe fruit* ***well sweet*** *and soon to burst.*

Elisa J. Sobo describing the Jamaican feminine ideal
from ***Many Mirrors****, 1994*

WOMEN'S BODIES IN OTHER CULTURES

The culture of the Middle East has been consistent in its admiration for voluptuous women for hundreds of years, though in the late 1990's I understand there is the beginning of a counter-movement towards slimmer figures. Remember that the word arabesque is used to describe things "that have about them an element of fantasy, graceful flourish, a preference for the ornate, and flowing, curving lines" (R. Sanders). The belly dance emphasizes stomach and hip development. Islamic art is profuse in its forms. The harem is obviously a world in which women are idle, and idleness tends toward weight gain. However, most women in the East are not maintained in luxurious lassitude, yet fullness has been the Arabic standard. Perhaps the severity of the desert, the straightness of its vistas, and the scarceness of plant and animal life make female abundance so appealing.

She had breasts which are like two perfume jars of ivory, lending their luster to the moon, a belly with folds like the folds of delicate, white Egyptian linen, leading to a waist, slender beyond imagining, over hips like hills of sand, which force her to sit, when she tries to rise, and awaken her when she sleeps.

The Arabian Nights

[She] must have a perfect waist, and must be plump and lusty...her neck strong, her bust and her belly large; her breasts must be full and firm, her belly in good proportion, and her navel well-developed and marked; the lower part of the belly is to be large...

Translated by Sir Richard Burton from ***The Perfumed Garden****, 1886*

She was very beautiful, even though her status as a singer was only second-rate. All the same, he was more interested in her as a woman than as a singer. She certainly was desirable. Her folds of flesh and fat would warm a chilly man during the bitter cold of winter, which was at hand.

Naguib Mahfouz from ***Palace Walk****, 1989*

PICTURE CREDITS

Cover	Tamara De Lempicka	"La Tunique Rose," 1927.
Half-title	Henri Matisse	"Dance," 1932.
Title	Fernand Léger	"Nudes Against a Red Background," 1923.
Copyright	Édouard Manet	"Seated Bather," c.1858-1860.
Contents	Aristide Maillol	Lithograph, 1948.
vi	Vilhelm Hammershøi	"Study of a Model, or Nude Female Model," 1889.
Preface	Aristide Maillol	Lithograph, 1948.
10	Unknown	Mexican Statuette, c. A.D. 1000.
11	Anders Zorn	"Loftsängen," 1919.
12	Pieter Paul Rubens	"The Three Graces," before 1628-1630.
13	Pierre-Auguste Renoir	"Blond Bather," 1881.
14	Cecil Beaton	"The Modern Venus," 1928.
15	A.E. Marty	Magazine cover, c.1920s.
16	John Held Jr.	"Flapper," 1952.
17	Lucas Cranach	"Venus and Cupid with Stolen Honey," c.1530s.
18	Lotte Wernekink	Fashion illustration, c.1920s.
19	Unknown	Fashion plate, c.1920s
20	Pierre Bonnard	"Nu en hauteur," 1906.
21	Giovanni Bellini	"Woman With a Mirror," 1510.
22	Albrecht Dürer	"Draughtsman Drawing a Nude," c.1538.
23	Piotr Williams	"Woman in a Window," c.1930s.
24	Jean-Auguste-Dominique Ingres	"Madame Moitessier," 1851.
25	Unknown	Movie poster, 1953.
26	Anders Zorn	"Margit," 1891.
27	Albert André	"Femme S'essuyant," 1909.
28	Adolph von Menzel	"Memory of Swinemünde," 1851.
29	Gustav Klimt	"Danaë," 1907-1908.
30	Charles Maurin	"Eve," 1897.
31	Janis Rozentals	"Ieva," 1910-1912.
32	Jan Gossaert	"Neptune and Amphitrite," 1516.
33	Gustav Klimt	"Adam and Eve," 1917-1918.
34	Rockwell Kent	"Venus and Adonis," 1931.
35	Pieter Paul Rubens	"Toilet of Venus," 1612-1615.
36	Guercino (Giovanni Francesco Barbieri)	"Venus, Mars and Cupid," 1634.
37	Tiziano Vecellio	"Venus and an Organist," 1549.
38	Lorenzo Di Credi	"Venus," c.1490.
39	Johann Liss	"Venus at her Mirror," c.1625.
40	Correggio	"The Three Graces," c.1518.
41	Poppi	"The Three Graces," c.1570.
42	Frederick Sandys	"Gentle Spring," c.1860.
43	Palma Vecchio	"Flora," 1522.
44	Luca Giordano.	"The Triumph of Galatea, with Acis Transformed into a Spring," c.1690.
45	Baron Antoine-Jean Gros	"Diana," 1791.
46	Unknown	Postcard, c.1910s.
47	Em. Dupuis	Postcard, c.1916.
47	Em. Dupuis	Postcard, c.1916.

PICTURE CREDITS

48	Unknown	Trade card, c.1890s.
49	Hans von Aachen	"Allegory of Peace, Art and Abundance," 1602.
50	Lord Leighton	"Flaming June," c.1895.
51	Diego Rivera.	"The Elements," 1926-1927.
52	Pierre-Paul Prud'hon.	"The French Constitution, Equality, Law," c.1791-1798.
53	Alphonse Mucha.	"Fruit," c.1897.
54	Guido Reni.	"Cleopatra," c.1630s.
55	Leon Bakst.	Costume design for Cleopatra, 1909.
56	Jean-Léon Gérôme.	"Bathsheba," 1889.
57	Maurice Denis.	"Bathsabee Au Bain Dans Les Jardins de Grenade," c.1905-1913.
58	Duane Bryers.	Hilda.
59		Hilda.
60		Hilda.
61		Hilda.
62	Rembrandt van Rijn	"Jupiter and Antiope," 1659.
63		"Bathshebe," 1654.
64		"Cleopatra," c.1640s.
65		"Saskia as Flora," 1634.
66	Pieter Paul Rubens	"Life Drawing of a Woman"
67		"Portrait of Isabella Brant," c.1625-1626.
68		"The Three Graces," c.1620-1623.
69		"Helena Fourment Putting on a Glove," c.1630.
70		"The Judgement of Paris," 1632-1635.
71		"Helena in a Fur Coat," c.1631.
72	Pierre-Auguste Renoir	"Psyche," 1895.
73		"Gabrielle with Jewelry," c.1910.
74		"Dancing Nude with Tambourine," c.1912.
75		"Bather Arranging her Hair," 1885.
76		"Bather Drying Herself," c.1885.
77		"Dancer with Castanets," 1909.
78		"Young Girl with a Rose," 1913.
79		"Bather Arranging Her Hair," 1885.
80		"Bathers (Grandes Baigneuses)," 1918-1919.
81		"After the Bath," 1910.
82	Boris Kustodiev	"Belle," 1915.
83		"The Merchant's Wife," 1918.
84		"Merchant's Wife," 1915.
85		"Russian Venus," 1926.
86		"A Sailor and his Sweetheart," 1921.
87		"Merchant's Wife Drinking Tea," 1923.
88	Aristide Maillol	Lithograph, 1948.
89		"Pomone aux Bras Tombants," c.1907.
90	Gaston Lachaise	"Walking Woman," 1922.
91		"Classic Torso," 1928.
92	Reginald Marsh	"Girl on a Merry go Round," 1946.
93		"Two Young Women Walking," 1944.
94	Pablo Picasso	"Women Running on the Beach," 1926.

PICTURE CREDITS

95	Pablo Picasso	"La Belle Hollandaise," 1905.
96		"Three Women at the Spring," 1921.
97		"Seated Nude Drying her Foot," 1921.
98	Unknown	Advertisement, c.1882.
99	Unknown	Postcard, c.1900s.
100	Stieborsky	Postcard, c.1920s.
101	Paul Krawutschke	"2me Exposition Suisse de l'Automobile," 1906.
102	Gian Emilio Malerba	"Mele," 1910.
103	Fernand Khnopff	"Etude de Femme," c.1890-1892.
104	Unknown	Advertisement, c.1890s.
105	Unknown	Magazine cover, 1904.
106	Unknown	Photograph of Marie Rôze, c.1880s.
107	Josef Engelhart	Magazine illustration, 1898.
108	Herman Mishkin	"Margaret Ober," 1913.
109		"Karin Banzell," c.1910s.
110	Félix Tournachon	"Chorus Girls at the Folies," c.1880.
111	Jules Alexandre Grün	Poster, 1900.
112	Reginald Marsh	"Star Burlesk," 1933.
113	Charles Lucien Léandre	"Laurence Deschampes," c.1901.
114	Unknown	Postcard, c.1890s.
115	The Snark	Annual cover, 1907.
116	Valdimir Lebedev	"A Girl in a Football Jersey with a Bunch of Flowers," 1933.
117	Hendrick ter Brugghen	"Ballad Singer," 1628.
118	Egisto Lancerotto	"A Young Woman in a Vineyard," c.1900.
119	Pierre-Auguste Renoir	"Summer," 1868.
120	Fernando Castro Pacheco	"Woman Striding," c.1940s.
121	Pierre-Auguste Renoir	"Maternity (Aline and Pierre Renoir)," 1886.
122	Gustav Vigeland	"Mother and Child," c.1928.
123	Kuzma Petrov-Vodkin	"Mother," 1915.
124	Henri Matisse	"Nude in Armchair," c.1906.
125	Jacopo Robusti Tintoretto	"Suzanne et les Vieillards," c.1550-1590.
126	Bartholomeus van Der Helst	"Anna du Pire as Granida," 1660.
127	Camille Bombois	"Nude with Raised Arms," 1925.
128	Tamara De Lempicka	"La Tunique Rose," 1927.
129	Jean Metzinger	"Woman with a Pheasant," 1926.
130	Antonio Dongh	"Washerwomen," 1922.
131	Unknown	Indian Fertility Goddess, Third Century, B.C.
132	Winifred Bruton	"Queen Nefert," 1936.
133	Félix Vallotton	"African Woman," 1910.
134	Unknown	Indian Rock Painting, Fifth Century, A.D.
135	Paul Gauguin	"The Moon and the Earth," 1893.
136	Unknown	Engraving, late Nineteenth Century.
137	Henri Matisse	"Odalisque with Grey Trousers," 1927.
138	Jean-Léon Gérôme	"Dance of the Almeh," 1863.
139	Jean-Auguste Dominique Ingres	"The Turkish Bath," 1832.
Colophon	Rockwell Kent	"Venus and Adonis," 1931.
Back cover	Fernand Léger	"Three Women," 1921.

BIBLIOGRAPHY

Beller, Anne Scott. Fat and Thin: A Natural History of Obesity. New York: Farrar, Straus and Giroux, 1977.
Bordo, Susan. Unbearable Weight: Feminism, Western Culture, and the Body. Berkeley: University of California Press, 1993.
Chernin, Kim. The Obsession: Reflections on the Tyranny of Slenderness. New York: Harper & Row, 1981.
Cichy, Bodo. Masterpeices of Figure Painting. New York: Crown Publishing, 1959.
Clark, Kenneth. The Nude: A Study in Ideal Form. New York: Bollingen Foundation, 1956.
Cooke, Kaz. Real Gorgeous: The Truth about Body and Beauty. New York: WW Norton, 1996.
Eisler, George. Naked to Nude: Life Drawing in the Twentieth Century. London: Thames & Hudson Ltd., 1977.
Garland, Madge. Beauty: Four Thousand Years of Beautiful Women. London: Weidenfeld and Nicolson, 1957.
Garland, Madge. The Changing Form of Fashion. New York: Praeger, 1970.
Lakoff, Robin Tolmach and Scherr, Raquel L. Face Value: The Politics of Beauty. Boston: Routledge, 1984.
Morris, Desmond. Bodywatching: A Field Guide to the Human Species. London: Jonathan Cape, 1985.
Nead, Lynda. The Female Nude: Art, Obscenity and Sexuality. London: Routledge, 1992.
Rudofsky, Bernard. The Unfashionable Human Body. New York: Doubleday, 1971.
Sobo, Elisa J. "The Sweetness of Fat." Many Mirrors: body Image and Social Relations. Piscatawat, NJ: Rutgers University Press, 1994.
Stearns, Peter N. Fat History: Bodies and Beauty in the Modern West. New York: New York University Press, 1997.
Steele, Frances Mary and Adams, Elizabeth Livingston Steele. Beauty of Form and Grace of Vesture. New York: Dodd, Mead and Company, 1892.
Steele, Valerie. Fashion and Eroticism: Ideals of Feminine Beauty From the Victorian Era to the Jazz Age. New York: Oxford University Press, 1985.
Walker, Alexander. Beauty. New York: J & H.G. Langley, 1843.
Warner, Marina. Monuments & Maidens: The Allegory of the Female Form. New York: Simon & Schuster, 1985.

ACKNOWLEDGEMENTS

Excerpt from The Female Nude: Art, Obscenity and Sexuality by Lynda Nead. Copyright " 1992 by Lynda Nead. Reprinted by permission of Routledge. Excerpts from Fat & Thin: A Natural History of Obseity by Anne Scott Beller. Copyright © 1977 by Anne Scott Beller. Reprinted by permission of Farrar, Straus & Giroux, Inc. Excerpt from What is Beauty? by Dorothy Schefer. Copyright © 1997 by Beauty Cares/ Hair Cares. Reprinted by permission of Universe Publishing. Excerpt from Bodywatching by Desmond Morris. Copyright © 1985 by Desmond Morris. Reprinted by permission of Jonathan Cape. Clark, Kenneth; The Nude: A Study in Ideal Form. Copyright © 1956 by The Trustees of the National Gallery of Art. Reprinted by permission of Princeton University Press. Princeton Bollingen Delux. Excerpts from Unbearable Weight: Feminism, Western Culture, and the Body by Susan Bordo. Copyright © 1993 by the Regents of the University of California Press. Reprinted by permission of the Regents of the University of California and the University of California Press.Excerpts as submitted from The Obsession: Reflections on the Tyranny of Slenderness by Kim Chernin. Copyright © 1981 by Kim Chernin. Reprinted by permission of HarperCollins Publishers, Inc. Excerpt from From Naked to Nude: Life Drawing in the Twentieth Century by George Eisler. Copyright © 1977 by George Eisler. Reprinted by permission of Thames & Hudson Ltd. Excerpt from "When it comes to Women and Bodies, God probably said: let there be flesh" by Demitria Martinez. © 1995. Reprinted by permission of the author. Excerpt from Face Value: The Politics of Beauty by Robin Tolmach Lafoff and Raquel L. Scherr. Copyright © 1984 by Robin Tolmach Lakoff and Raquel L. Scherr. Reprinted by permission of International Thomson Publishing Services. Excerpt from Monuments & Maidens: the Allegory of Female Form by Marina Warner. Copyright © 1985 by Marina Warner. Reprinted by permission of Scribner, a Division of Simon & Schuster. Excerpt from Masterpieces of Figure Painting by Bodo Cichy. Copyright © 1959 by Bodo Cichy. Reprinted by permission of The Crown Publishing Group. Excerpt from Boris Kustodiev: The Artist and His Work by Victoria Lebedeva. Copyright © 1981 by Progress Publishers. Reprinted by permission of the publisher. Excerpt from Aristide Maillol by Bertrand Lorquin. Copyright © 1994 by Editions d'Art Albert Skira S.A. Reprinted by permission of Editions d'Art Albert Skira S.A. Excerpt from Reginald Marsh's New York: Paintings, Drawings, Prints and Photographs by Marilyn Cohen. Copyright ©1983 by the Whitney Museum of American Art. Reprinted by permission of the publisher. From The Unfashionable Human Body by Bernard Rudofsky. Copyright © 1971 by Bernard Rudofsky. Used by permission of Doubleday, a division of Random House, Inc. Excerpt from On Classic Ground: Picasso, Léger, de Chirico and the New Classicism 1910–1930 by Elizabeth Cowling and Jennifer Mundy. Copyright © 1990 by The Tate Gallery. Reprinted by permission of the publisher. Excerpts from Fashion and Eroticism: Ideals of Feminine Beauty from the Victorian Era to the Jazz Age by Valerie Steele. Copyright © 1985 by the Oxford University Press, Inc. Reprinted by permission of the author. Excerpts from Fat History: Bodies and Beauty in the Modern West by Peter N. Stearns. Copyright © 1997 by New York University. Reprinted by permission of the New York University Press. Excerpt from The Queen's Throat: Opear, Homosexuality, and the Mystery of Desire by Wayne Koestenbaum. Copyright © 1993 by Wayne Koestenbaum. Reprinted by permission of Simon & Schuster. Excerpt from Paris 1900: Masterworks of French Poster Art by Hermann Schardt. Copyright © 1970 by Chr. Belser Verlag. Reprinted by permission of Penguin Putnam. Excerpt from Two-Headed Woman by Lucille Clifton. Copyright © 1980 by The University of Massachusetts Press. Reprinted by permission of the author. Excerpt from Many Mirrors: Body Image and Social Relations edited by Nicole Sault. Copyright © 1994 by Rutgers, The State University. Used by permission of Rutgers University Press. Excerpt from Palace Walk by Naguib Mahfouz. Copyright © 1956 by The American University in Cairo Press. Reprinted by permission of the publisher. We have been unable to discover the copyright holders of several of the works in this book, and hope to hear from them so that we can arrange to credit them in future printings.

THIS BOOK WAS TYPESET IN CASLON

BOOK DESIGN BY SACHEVERELL DARLING AT BLUE LANTERN STUDIO

PRINTED IN SINGAPORE BY STAR STANDARD